THE CHILDREN
TRAP

Other books by Robert L. Thoburn

*How To Establish and Operate
a Successful Christian School*, 1975

The Christian and Politics, 1984

THE CHILDREN TRAP

The Biblical Blueprint for Education

Robert L. Thoburn

DOMINION PRESS • FT. WORTH, TEXAS

THOMAS NELSON, INC. • NASHVILLE • CAMDEN • NEW YORK

Co-published by Dominion Press, Ft. Worth, Texas, and Thomas Nelson, Inc., Nashville, Tennessee.

Typesetting by Thoburn Press, Tyler, Texas

Printed in the United States of America

Unless otherwise noted, all Scripture quotations are from the New King James Version of the Bible, copyrighted 1984 by Thomas Nelson, Inc., Nashville, Tennessee.

Library of Congress Catalog Card Number 86-050789

ISBN 0-930462-22-8

TABLE OF CONTENTS

EDITOR'S INTRODUCTION
by Gary North

Meeting with a group of Christians in Austin [Texas] on May 19, 1986, [Attorney General James] Mattox revealed his true colors when asked, *"Is it true that the State of Texas owns our children?"* Mattox retorted, *"Yes, it is true . . . and not only your children, but you, too!"*[1]

Hard to believe, isn't it? Yet this is an ancient view in the United States. John Swett served as California's Superintendent of Public Instruction from 1863 to 1868. In 1864, he published the *First Biennial Report* of his office. He cited favorably several judicial decisions in eastern states. Among them was this:

> *Parents have no remedy as against the teacher*—As a general thing, the only persons who have a legal right to give orders to the teacher, are his employers—namely, the committee in some States, and in others the Director of Trustees. If his conduct is approved of by his employees, the parents have no remedy as against him or them. . . .[2]

"On March 28, 1874, the California Legislature made it a penal offense for parents to send their children to private schools without the consent of the local state school trustees."[3]

How did Christian parents allow themselves to be swept into supporting the public school movement? Why do they still continue to support it financially and verbally? Why haven't they risen up in political revenge against anyone who proposes tax financing of education, a public school monopoly, or state-imposed

---

1. *Texans Against Compromise in Education* (July 18, 1986).
2. Cited by R. J. Rushdoony, *The Messianic Character of American Education* (Nutley, New Jersey: Craig Press, 1963), p. 81.
3. *Idem.*

standards on Christian schools? I have three answers. First, because they have believed a lie, that the state is responsible for educating children. Second, because they are cheap, and foolishly seek to compel other people to pay for the education of Christian children. Third, because they have believed Satan's number-one lie, the myth of neutrality.

Building the Pen

There is the story of a hunter who year after year kept bringing to market huge quantities of wild boar. Nobody could figure out how he did it. He never told his secret. Finally, on his deathbed, some of his friends asked him how he had done it.

"Well, it took a lot of planning. First, I set out troughs of food. The older hogs refuse to get near it at first, but the younger ones do come sniffing around, and they eventually start eating. I let them do this for about a month. Even the older boars start joining the younger ones at the trough. Then I build a fence behind the trough. This scares them at first, but they find it easier to eat here than forage for themselves, so they come back. Then I build a second fence at a 90-degree angle to the back fence. That takes them a while to get used to, but they eventually do. Then comes the third side, and then the back side. There's a large gate in that final strip of fencing, and it's always wide open. It's on hinges. The hogs keep coming. After all, it's free food for one and all. When enough of them come in for their free food, I just shut the gate. The rest is easy."

This is precisely the strategy used by God-hating humanists against Christians. The free food is called "free education." But the humanists are even smarter than that hunter. They make the adult Christian hogs pay for the fencing and the humanist slop in the trough. This system is called taxation. The short-sighted pigs pay for the slaughter of their own offspring. Pigs love their free slop, even when it isn't free. Warn them that the slop in the trough is a trap for their piglets, and you will hear a lot of outraged squealing. You will make a lot of enemies.

Robert Thoburn will make a lot of enemies with this book.

The Myth of Neutrality

What has been the most successful lie in the history of Christianity? There can be no doubt: *the myth of neutrality.* This myth has kept Christians for two thousand years from developing explicitly and exclusively Biblical solutions to their problems. They have returned, generation after generation, to Greek, Roman, and modern philosophy and institutions, on the assumption that God and Satan, good and evil, Christians and non-Christians share certain fundamental beliefs, or at least share certain views of the world around them. But they don't. Every fact is an *interpreted* fact. Satan interprets the world in his way, while God interprets it in another. Satan sees this world as rightfully his, not God's; God sees it as rightfully his, not Satan's. There can be no reconciliation between these two views. All attempts at reconciling them necessarily lead to Satan's view: that God has no right to tell us how to interpret His world.

There is no neutrality. There may be indifference. A person may not care which athletic team wins a game, but he cannot be neutral about whose creation has made possible the game. Neutrality is the devil's most successful myth. He used it on Eve. He persuaded her to become a neutral experimenter. She could test God's word, to see whether or not she would die on the day she ate the fruit. "Just a neutral scientific experiment," he implied. "What have you got to lose?" The answer: *everything*.

The modern institution that is most self-consciously built in terms of the myth of neutrality is the "public" school, meaning the *government* school, meaning the *taxpayer-financed* school. Its legal foundation is the myth of neutrality. No religious or sectarian views are supposed to be taught in a public school, because people of many different religious beliefs are required by law to support it financially. Expenditures of tax money are supposed to be neutral, non-religious expenditures.

All this talk of neutral education is sheer nonsense. You cannot teach without ultimate concepts of true and false. Label one idea false—the evolution of the universe out of random matter that exploded with a big bang 15 billion years ago—and you have attacked some taxpayer's deeply held religious convictions. Label another idea true—the evolution of mankind from lower animals, for example—and you have attacked a different taypayer's deeply held religious view. You are using his money to indoctrinate his children with ideas that he despises. Without exception, the major victims today are conservative Christians whose children are under deliberate religious and intellectual attack by taxpayer-financed schools.

This has been going on at Christian taxpayers' expense for over a century, with nary a squeal of protest from the victims, certainly not from the 1925 Scopes "monkey trial" in Dayton, Tennessee until the mid-1960's, when the independent (non-parochial) Christian school movement began to revive.

Why have Christians gone along with this obvious confidence game? Three reasons. First and foremost, because they had already bought the myth of socialist education, namely, that it is the moral and financial responsibility of the state to educate children, not the moral and financial responsibility of parents.

Second, Christians want their religion, but they want it cheap. They refuse to tithe to the church, so they wind up tithing (and paying far more than ten percent) to the state. They have *tithed their children* to the state! "Free education! Free education!" The pigs have sent their offspring to the slaughter for well over a century.

Third, Christians have been afraid to deny the myth of neutrality in the fields of politics and civil law. They have feared becoming labeled "theocrats" by their God-hating enemies, so they have bought the party line regarding neutrality. The party line is the humanist party line. They bought it first with respect to civil law, so it was an easy step for the humanists to sell it to them in the field of education.

Civil Law

Every law is religious. Every law tells certain people that they are not allowed to do certain things, or that they must do other things. Every law is based on an idea of *right* vs. *wrong*. Right and wrong are therefore moral concepts, and all morality is religious. But the myth of so-called natural law — common law, common morality — has done its work in the field of civil law. Christians do not look to God's revelation in the Bible to tell them what kinds of laws are legitimate and which kinds are not. So Christians have abandoned law and politics to their rivals, who also operate in terms of a religion — the religion of humanism, which is defended everywhere in terms of the myth of neutrality.

Is there neutrality between heaven and hell? Will those in hell have a vote in what happens in heaven? Will God give "equal time to Satan" throughout eternity? Should Christians be required to allow atheists to have equal time in the pulpit each Sunday? If Christians do not want the problem of "equal time for Satan" to arise, they must start limiting the state. They must start voting to limit the money that the state can tax and spend on state-approved projects.

Everything on earth is a battle between the principles of the Bible and anti-Biblical principles. A war is in progress. But Christians have refused to face this fact for well over a century in the field of education. It would involve giving up "free" humanist slop in the trough.

Nowhere is this war more clearly in progress than in the battle for the minds of men. And the major battlefield is the field of tax-payer-financed education. Men are battling for the loyalty and obedience of the next generation. And for a hundred years, Christians have been losing the battle. Why? Because they have decided to grant to their rivals the fundamental point: the myth of neutrality. They have accepted as morally valid — indeed, morally preferable — the tax-supported compulsory school. Since the 1840's in the United States, this institution has been the targeted prize of God-hating, humanist kidnappers, beginning with Massachusetts' Horace Mann, who used the God-hating, man-deifying, evil school system of apostate Prussia as his model for the public schools.

Christians want their education, but they want it cheap. So it nas cost them almost everything, just as it cost Eve.

Reforming the Public Schools

All is not lost, most Christians tell us. "We can and must reform the public schools!" (Have we seen anything but academic and moral decline since 1840?) "We can and must make them safe again." (Teachers get mugged; over 70% of the students have experimented with drugs before graduation; Planned Parenthood is allowed on many campuses, teaching abortion as a legitimate alternative.) "We can force them to teach creationism." (Does any school district in the United States teach it?) "The public school creationist view will not mention a Creator, of course; that would be illegal, a violation of the myth of neutrality." (Creationism without a Creator?) "But we can teach a zero-God view of creationism." And then Christians are asked to contribute hundreds of thousands of dollars — money that could be building Christian schools — in attorney fees to fight these "Creation science" cases, *not one of which has been won*, and not one of which is likely to be won.

Or what about this one? "We'll get prayer back into the schools!" The prayer can't mention Jesus, of course. That would violate the myth of neutrality, and we all believe in the separation of church (whose God is decidedly unneutral) and state. But the prayer can at least mention the word "God." Only it can't. Not one school district in the nation *legally* can permit such prayer. Only silent prayer is allowed. So much for freedom of religion. What the U.S. Congress has every morning — prayer by a taxpayer-financed chaplain — children are not entitled to.

The Arguments for "Staying in the System"

You have heard lots of arguments for Christians sending their children to the public schools, and for running these schools on a Biblical, moral basis. Let me list a few:

1. We need to regulate the public schools.
2. We need to inspect them for health.
3. We need to make them safe from violence.
4. We need to require a prayer when they begin. (Illegal?)
5. Well, we need to have them allow *voluntary* prayer before they begin. (Illegal?)

6. Well, then, each student should be allowed to offer a silent prayer before he begins school. After all, this is a Christian nation!

7. Christian children need to attend. They need to be exposed early to the real world; they shouldn't be kept in religious hothouses.

Let me try an analogy on you. We are adults here. Substitute the word "whorehouses" for "public schools." Now, let's hear these same familiar arguments in favor of making the public schools decent for Christians:

1. We need to regulate the local whorehouses.

2. We need to inspect them for disease.

3. We need to make them safe from violence.

4. We need to require a prayer when they open for business. (Illegal?)

5. Well, we need to have them allow *voluntary* prayer before they open for business. (Illegal?)

6. Well, then, each customer should be allowed to offer a silent prayer before he conducts his business. After all, this is a Christian nation!

7. Christian children need to be exposed early to the real world; they shouldn't be kept in religious hothouses. ("Cathouses, not hothouses!")

Preposterous, aren't they? But if the myth of neutrality is false, then equally preposterous are all the calls to "recapture our public schools." They were never "ours" in the first place. They inherently violate Biblical principles: the family has the moral and financial responsibility for educating its children, not the state.

But is a public school the same as a whorehouse? It's close enough! God calls worshipping false gods "whoring after false gods." False worship is whoredom, and whoredom is the worship of false gods. The two are equated in the Bible. The Book of Hosea is built around this theme.

What is a school system that teaches mankind's evolution out of meaningless slime, if not whoredom? What is a school system that makes it illegal to teach God's law as the only valid moral standard for mankind, if not whoredom? What is a school system that the U.S. Supreme Court says is not even allowed to post the Ten Commandments on a wall in the classroom, if not whoredom? What is a school system that teaches that the Bible is *not* a God-inspired book, but at best "literature" — no better than Shakespeare's plays, Hemingway's novels, or for that matter, the Marquis de Sade's novels? Everything is relative, after all, says the myth of neutrality.

All right, I am exaggerating. I admit it. Whorehouses really aren't like public schools. There is a fundamental difference between whorehouses and public schools: *whorehouses aren't tax-supported*. They aren't compulsory, either. We don't have elections for the State Superintendent of Public Brothels.

But, some tuition-avoiding Christian parents may protest, our children do not necessarily believe everything their public school teachers tell them for twelve years (or sixteen, or twenty), eight hours a day, five days a week, eight months a year, plus homework. No, *our* children will believe what *we* tell them (after they spend three hours a day watching television), and what they learn in church on Sunday. This is the equivalent of arguing that it is safe to send your children into a whorehouse for twelve years to learn music appreciation from the piano player. (After all, he's a "professor"!) Are we to believe that moral atmosphere and moral temptations count for nothing? Of course they count. Then how can any Christian believe that the public school environment counts for nothing?

They don't believe it; they just *say* they believe it. They are simply too cheap before God to pull their children out of the system. They prefer to send their children daily into an education system designed in the pits of hell rather than sacrifice their summer vacation trip or be forced to move into a smaller home. They prefer to talk endlessly about "cleaning up the public schools someday," while sitting quietly, doing nothing except paying ever-higher property tax bills, and wailing about how great the schools used to be when they were in school. Like the ex-slaves wandering in the wilderness and fearful of entering Canaan, they delude themselves with false memories of the leeks and onions of Egypt.

They would prefer to dream about a mythical political program to "clean up Egypt" rather than conquering Canaan.

The Separation of School and State

This book is a detailed study of the Biblical view of education in contrast to the humanist view. The author concludes that we must insist on the separation of school and state. The state is not to be trusted with the shaping of the minds of the voters. Getting the state out of education at every level is the *only* way to achieve God-honoring education.

It is not the state's function to support the educational establishment. If it does, this is the equivalent of *state-supported religious worship*. It is the re-establishment (compulsory tax-financing) of the church, with a new priesthood, the teachers.

Established Churches

The public schools have long been America's only established church. This has been recognized by liberal church historian Sidney Mead and by conservative scholar R. J. Rushdoony. In 1963, Mead wrote this brilliant analysis of the Christian dilemma over public schools — a dilemma that has yet to be resolved, but which Christians need to resolve once and for all. There was a time in U.S. history when churches were established (paid for) by the state. This ended in the nineteenth century. But when the churches gave up state support in order to secure religious freedom, they lost something very important, Mead says: power over the schools.

> Perhaps the most striking power that the churches surrendered under religious freedom was control over public education which traditionally had been considered an essential aspect of the work of an established church if it was to perform its proper function of disseminating and inculcating the necessary foundational religious beliefs. . . .[4]

---

4. Sidney E. Mead, *The Lively Experiment: The Shaping of Christianity in America* (New York: Harper & Row, 1963), p. 66.

And who can deny that these beliefs are religious? Certainly this was clearly recognized by early leaders such as Horace Mann, who frankly stood for "nonsectarian" religious teaching in the public schools. But it was soon discovered that there could be no "nonsectarian" religious teaching in America, because religion had been poured into sectarian molds and had hardened into sectarian forms. Thus Horace Mann's brand seemed to many evangelical Protestants to be suspiciously "Unitarian," and at best what passed as "nonsectarian" religious teaching seemed to many Unitarians, Roman Catholics, and others to be evangelical Protestantism. Even the Bible was ruled out, for it could not be read in the public schools except in "sectarian" English translations.

Here are the roots of the dilemma posed by the acceptance of the practice of separation of church and state on the one hand, and the general acceptance of compulsory public education sponsored by the state on the other. Here is the nub of the matter that is all too often completely overlooked. . . .[5]

In other words, the public schools in the United States took over one of the basic responsibilities that traditionally was always assumed by an established church. In this sense the public-school system of the United States *is* its established church But the situation in America is such that none of the many religious sects can admit without jeopardizing its existence that the religion taught in the schools (or taught in any other sect for that matter) is "true" in the sense that it can legitimately claim supreme allegiance. This serves to accentuate the dichotomy between the religion of the nation inculcated by the state through public schools, and the religion of the denominations taught in the free churches.[6]

In that same year, 1963, Rushdoony wrote:

The extensive emphasis on moralism and patriotism in state-supported schools was in fulfilment of this purpose in their creation, to become the "catholic" [universal] church of the people of America and the moral identity of the body politic. This aspect of educational history is in abundant evidence; it has been neglected

---

5. *Ibid.*, p. 67.
6. *Ibid.*, p. 68.

only because, while latter-day Puritans helped powerfully to make state support a reality, the schools fell steadily into the hands of the anti-Puritans. As a result, the school continues today as the true established church of the United States, dedicated to a catholic faith which is no longer semi-Christian moralism but social morality and social democracy.[7]

Christians who would not tolerate for a moment the idea of state-supported compulsory churches are strong supporters of state-supported compulsory education. They are intellectually schizophrenic.

What will drive Christians out of the public schools? Not heterosexual venereal disease, which is rampant on high school campuses. Not drugs; over 70% of all high school students have experimented with them. Not violence in the classroom, which is universally acknowledged by educators as a problem. Not interracial busing (though this drives out some parents, and not just Christians). What will it take? An outbreak of AIDS? Not even that, I suspect, though possibly.

In Texas, only one thing could do it: ten consecutive years of tie football scores, especially zero to zero. Then Christian parents would listen. This—and only this—would be seen as a true judgment of God.

If every Baptist family in the American South would refuse to put its children into the public schools this year, the whole public school system would collapse overnight. This is the power implicitly held by Christians. But they are pagans at heart, and furthermore, about half the time their local football teams win. The Christians stay put.

This book will anger them.

Which Kind of Structure

This book will also bother defenders of Christian schools. It shows that the most effective structure of Christian education is the *profit-seeking, tax-paying, privately owned school*. This system

---

7. R. J. Rushdoony, *The Messianic Character of American Education*, pp. 44-45.

transfers the greatest sovereignty to parents, yet it also makes possible the division of labor.

This conclusion will upset the more vocal defenders of home schooling, whose schools rarely can make full use of the division of labor, especially at the high school level. It will also upset the defenders of non-profit, board-operated ("parent-controlled") schools. Such schools are far more bureaucratic than profit-seeking schools, since the operators do not get to keep the profits personally. Such board-operated, "parent-run" schools eventually are run by parents of adult children who have long since graduated, not the parents of the presently enrolled students. So "parent-run boards" are a misnomer. The only absolutely parent-run school is a home school. There can be parent-influenced schools, but to call a non-profit bureaucracy a parent-run school prejudices the case.

This book finally challenges the idea of church-run schools, for these schools always seek indirect subsidies — financial or space — from church members whose children are not enrolled, or who have no children, or who have a rival approach to education. These schools generally place too much responsibility on pastors, who are not being paid to administer a school. Church-run schools bring dissension into the church. They invariably reduce the influence of the parents of enrolled students, to the extent of the indirect subsidies being paid by other people.

It would be far better to have a family-owned, profit-seeking school next door to a sponsoring church, with the church renting the school's facilities in the evenings and on weekends. But then what happens if another family in the church wants to start a school (competition for the first school), but cannot get the same subsidy? Once again, you get avoidable dissension in the church.

The solution is freedom. The answer is free market competition. The answer is the principle of the market: *something for something*. The answer is: parents should pay the full costs of educating their own children, the same way they buy food, shelter, haircuts, Christmas presents, and just about everything else. The answer is: *no more compulsory subsidies — either in God's name or the state's*.

Perhaps some church members really cannot afford to send

their children to private Christian schools. Let them request financial aid. Let the deacons examine the family's finances. Let them suggest ways of cutting back on expenses. If the family still cannot afford it, let the deacons use church funds to finance a partial scholarship. Charity should go to those who need it, not to those who don't (as is the case when the church runs the school and charges below-cost tuitions to every family).

Let the churches raise money for needy students through voluntary, tax-deductible donations to a church-operated scholarship fund. Then let the parents decide which Christian school to send their children to. The church should support parents directly and schools indirectly, not schools directly and parents indirectly. This maintains the Biblical principle of parental responsibility for education, with the church as a defender of *families*, not educators.

After you finish this book, you will understand this principle far better.

Part I
BLUEPRINTS

When a world disintegrates, nothing more quickly becomes contemptible than its dead values, nothing more dead than its fallen gods, and nothing more offensively fetid than its old necessities. This will be no less true of the values of this dying age, of which one of the chiefest is the statist school. If the new order is capable of breaking with statism, it will in due course turn on every citadel of statism, the school no less than any other. At present, nothing seems more unlikely, although straws in the wind indicate the direction of the present temper. . . .

But much more is involved. The state school is radically involved in the contemporary culture, both as a product thereof and its champion. In spite of adverse trends, it will survive as long as the culture survives, and no longer. To this culture, a compulsory state religion seems radically wrong, but not a compulsory state education. But between the two no real difference exists; both require the compulsive power of the state for whatever the culture deems necessary. Compulsion in religion was in an earlier era a social necessity, even as it now is in education. The cause of religion then required compulsion, even as the cause of education now requires compulsion and the state. In both instances, compulsion has been productive of very marked gains of a sort and of heavy penalties as well. But that education may play an even more important role in another age by no means requires that education be statist in even the slightest degree. Statist education will remain, for all the vehemence of the attacks on it, and will increase its reliance on and subservience to the state, as long as the contemporary culture remains, but, with the collapse of that culture, the education of that culture will rapidly wither away. And we are at the end of an age, in an era turning rapidly on itself and looking vainly thus far for a new sense of direction.

R. J. Rushdoony*

*Rushdoony, *Intellectual Schizophrenia* (Phillipsburg, NJ: The Presbyterian and Reformed Publishing Company, 1961), pp. 112-13.

INTRODUCTION

This is a book for slow learners. Not children . . . parents. Specifically, it is a book for Christian parents.

For well over a century, Christians have refused to face the facts about public education, meaning government education, meaning taxpayer-financed education. These days, the facts are on the front pages of the daily newspapers.

"POMERANTZ GETS 25 YEARS FOR SEX CRIMES"

This is the headline that appeared in a Northern Virginia newspaper on March 17, 1986. The article begins, "A Fairfax Circuit Court judge has sentenced former school psychologist Arthur S. Pomerantz to 25 years in prison for sex crimes involving teenage boys."

· The school system that Arthur S. Pomerantz served as a psychologist was none other than the Fairfax County Public Schools, one of the largest and most respected public school systems in the United States.

According to the article, "Pomerantz began working for the Fairfax County schools in 1965 and resigned in 1984. After his arrest, school officials admitted they knew Pomerantz had been the target of a juvenile sex investigation as early as 1981, but allowed him to keep his job because no criminal charges had been filed."

"CHICAGO TEACHERS TO BE FINGERPRINTED"

I didn't see that headline, but I heard on the radio a few nights ago that the Chicago school system wants to fingerprint all their teachers. They want to find out whether any of them have a criminal record. The report is that several of them have turned out to be child molesters.

CHRISTIAN PARENTS! It is one o'clock in the afternoon. Do you know who is "counselling" your little boy? Do you know what your seven year old daughter is being taught?

Is there a crisis in the public schools? You bet there is. Last night I saw some inner city kids on TV talking about the violence in the schools. They want to do something about the guns in the classrooms. One of them said, "I don't need a gun! I've got my fists!"

The crisis is moral. God is out so guns are in. Prayer is out so profanity and permissiveness are in.

Last week the Rev. Jesse Jackson spoke at our local high school for two hours. He invited those who had used dope to come down to the "altar" to confess. The teachers and counsellors expressed surprise that so many came. A vast majority!

The public schools are going to pot, literally. And to cocaine, and PCP, and whatever. As one lady whose kids attended the public schools put it to me quite bluntly and accurately, **"Public schools stink!"** I didn't say it. She did. She spoke from experience.

This is where taxpayer-financed education has led us. Yet it was originally preached by its promoters as a way to make people righteous, a way to save the world.

"IF YOU CAN READ THIS, THANK A TEACHER"

That's what a local bumper sticker says. I've thought of changing it in various ways. For instance, "If you can't read this, blame a teacher."

The sad thing is that all too many cannot read the bumper sticker. We're told there are 26 million adult Americans who cannot read or write at all. The National Institute of Education says that 47% of 17 year old minority youths are illiterate and that 60% of inmates in correctional institutions are unable to read.

Obviously there is an academic crisis in education today.

The fault lies with the system, no matter how much they try to put the blame elsewhere. Jacques Barzun, who spent 48 years at Columbia, states in his *Teacher in America*, "The once proud and efficient public-school system of the United States—especially its unique free high school for all—has turned into a wasteland where violence and vice share the time with ignorance and idleness, besides serving as battleground for vested interests, social, political, and economic."

To Light a Candle

God tells us in the Bible that we will reap what we sow. I do not need to belabor the point that the public schools in America are bad, and getting worse. They are getting plenty of criticism from within the system. I am not surprised that public school teachers frequently send their own children to Christian schools.

I am not going to write another book bashing the public school system. Nor am I interested in reforming the public schools. That is a waste of time. I decided a long time ago that it is better to light one little candle than to curse the darkness.

My interest is in the establishment of Christian schools throughout the world and the eventual abolition of all public schools. This is based on the conviction that the *only* solution to the moral and academic crises in education is a system of education based on the Word of God. "Unless the LORD builds the house, They labor in vain who build it." (Psalm 127:1)

The most important issue in education today involves the question of *control*. The question of control centers on the matter of responsibility. Just who is responsible for education?

The other issue has to do with the content of education. What is the purpose of education? How does a Christian education differ from a public school education?

Humanists Have Always Been In Control

"The teachers are in charge of the classrooms, the students control the restrooms, and the halls are a no-man's land." That is the way a public school board member in a wealthy suburban county described one large junior-senior high school.

The question, "Who should control education?" is the major issue in education today. The battles in the courts, in the legislatures, and before zoning boards all center around the issue of control.

The legal battles are recent, but the issues have been with us since the early 1800's. Some parents may think back fondly to "the good old days," when "good people ran good public schools." That memory is as mythical as the wilderness Hebrews' memory of the leeks and onions in Egypt. They had been in slavery, but they remembered only the occasional benefits.

The "Egyptians" deliberately designed the American public school system to be the primary means of enslaving Christians and reducing their cultural influence, by taking "professional" control over education of Christian children at the expense of their parents as taxpayers. Anyone who doubts this statement needs to read R. J. Rushdoony's book, *The Messianic Character of American Education* (1963), especially the chapter on the founder of modern public education in America, Horace Mann. They openly admitted what they were doing in their own books and their "professional journals."

When I was a kid in elementary school (what we called "grade school" in eastern Ohio), I knew who was in charge. I thought of the school as a jail. I would have understood the title of William F. Rickenbacker's book, *The Twelve-Year Sentence*. We kids were taught to dread the real jail where we were told the prisoners were given only bread and water. I did well in school, but I always looked upon the school as a jail because we were required to go there. I knew my parents would be in trouble if I didn't go to school.

The government had a man who showed up from time to time to check on our attendance at school. He was called the truant officer. I knew him as the "troll officer." That's what it sounded like to me. I had read about trolls in a reading book and I knew they were bad guys.

The government was firmly in charge of our education. Our local Presbyterian preacher (who didn't believe the Bible was the infallible Word of God) came in to teach a religion class once a week. That was the old "released time" system of allowing "religion" to be taught in the schools. The Supreme Court later made "released time" in public school buildings illegal. But religion was always being taught in the schools. Our principal was never seen to darken the door of a church. He said in class that human beings were like cows or dogs. When they were dead, that was the end of them.

This was my introduction to two major issues in education. 1) Who is in control? 2) What is going to be taught in the schools?

I learned about humanism at an early age. I became a humanist. I decided at age 13 to become a minister. I was idealistic. I wanted to help people. But I was a humanist just the same. I went on to a humanistic high school, then to a humanistic "Christian" college. In grade school and high school no one challenged the humanism. Everyone just seemed to accept it. It was the normal way to believe. No one ever suggested there might be a contradiction between Christianity and humanism.

The Bible Is Our Starting Point

I am writing this book to the tens of millions of persons in the United States who claim to believe in the Bible from cover to cover. Peter says, "For the time has come for judgment to begin at the house of God" (I Peter 4:17). I conclude that education also must begin with the house of God.

We cannot change the hearts of others. We can witness to them by our words and our actions. Only God can change them. As those who have been redeemed by the blood of Christ, we can determine how we are going to live.

I believe the three major problems in education are *humanism, humanism* and *humanism.* The sad fact is that much of the humanism is right in the church, among God's people.

What is humanism?

Put simply, *humanism is the worship of man.* Paul speaks of those who worship and serve the creature rather than the Creator.

The Creator/creature distinction is the most basic distinction there is. God is the Creator. He is Sovereign. He rules over all. He has made all things out of nothing. He is self-sufficient. Man, on the other hand, is a creature. He is dependent on his Creator.

In this book, I hope to convince you that parents are responsible for the education of their children and that education is to be God-centered. I will write from experience. I will cite facts. I will use reason. I may come up with a hundred and one different ways to try to convince you. But in the last analysis, the only case I can make is from Scripture.

The ultimate authority for all things is God. God has revealed Himself in two ways. One is natural revelation. The other is supernatural revelation.

Natural revelation is God's revelation in nature. "The heavens declare the glory of God; and the firmament shows His handiwork. Day unto day utters speech, and night unto night reveals knowledge" (Psalm 19:1-2).

The design of a snowflake reveals God. The regular appearance of Halley's Comet reveals God. The seasons, the transition from day to night reveal God. All the world knows that God exists, but as Paul says, "because, although they knew God, they did not glorifiy Him as God" (Romans 1:21).

What Paul is saying is that the non-believer has a revelation from God, but he chooses to worship man instead. That is humanism. The other way in which God makes Himself known is by supernatural revelation. Natural revelation is sometimes called general revelation because it comes to everyone in the world. Supernatural revelation is referred to as special revelation because it comes to a special people, the saved. God has preserved His supernatural or special revelation for us in the Bible.

The Bible is God's Word. It is true. The Scriptures are profitable for all things. The Bible is a lamp to our feet and a light to our path (Psalm 119:105). The Bible is our authority. The Bible is perfect. It is without error. The Bible is infallible. It can not be wrong.

I want to show from the Bible what the principles are that should guide us in education. If we depart from the Bible and argue on other grounds, then we are taking the humanist position. The authority for the humanist is man. The humanist may base his position on man in some collective form such as the state (civil government). He may argue from philosophy, psychology, sociology, experience, history, or whatever. He may even invoke the Constitution or some law or laws of man. It will always boil down to one thing—man.

The Great Debate in Education

The humanist will say the Christian is "authoritarian." The humanist is authoritarian also. He has his god and that god is man. He has humanistic laws, humanistic methods, and humanistic goals. The humanist is also religious. Man is inescapably religious. Humanism is the religion of the humanist.

Our starting point in life is all important. If we start with God and His Word, we will look at all of life in one way. If we start with man, we will look at life in a far different way.

1

GOD OWNS THE CHILDREN

The earth is the LORD's, and all its fullness, The world, and those that dwell therein" (Psalm 24:1).

A few years ago, a fierce battle broke out in the state of Ohio between the government and the Christian schools. The government authorities appealed to the Ohio State Constitution, which says that the state has a claim over children prior to the claims of parents.

In contrast, ancient societies held that children belonged to the parents. It was not unusual for female infants to be exposed to the elements and left to die. Males infants were seen as more important because the state needed warriors. Parents could kill their own children if they wished. This was true in "sophisticated" Rome.

Which is it? Do children belong to the state or the parents?

The Bible teaches that neither view is valid. Both positions are humanistic to the core. In America today, a woman is permitted by the state to put her unborn child to death. The practice of abortion has been legalized by the Supreme Court of the United States since 1973. The fact that the unborn child is referred to as a "fetus" or the "product of conception" does not change the situation one bit. The taking of the child's life may be called a surgical "procedure," but it is murder just the same

The humanist position has no regard for the sanctity of human life. It respects only presently held power: the power of the existing state or the existing parents to exercise their power over those who are presently defenseless. Its implications are frightening.

11

If children belong to parents, then parents can do whatever they want to do with them. Thus, child abuse is on the increase. Abortion, the ultimate in child abuse, ravages our land in epidemic proportions. It should not surprise us then that our schools are full of child abuse and violent children. On the other hand, if children belong to the state, then the state can do whatever it wants to do with them. The state can take them away from their parents at whatever age it wishes. The state can dictate whether they go to school, where they will go to school, and what they will be taught.

Clearly, the notion that either parents or the state ultimately owns the children is directly contrary to what the Bible teaches.

Children (Like Everything Else) Belong to God

Children are not made in the image of Caesar, so they do not belong to Caesar. Neither are they simply a bundle of shared genes and chromosomes, made in the image of their parents. They are *created* in the likeness of God. Every person on earth is made in the image of God. In the beginning God created the heavens and the earth—the totality of things (Genesis 1:1).

In Genesis 1:27 we read, "So God created man in His own image; in the image of God He created him; male and female He created them."

The image of God in man was not destroyed by the Fall of man into sin. After the Fall of Adam, God instituted the death penalty for the deliberate taking of human life. The reason God gave for the death penalty was that "in the image of God He made man" (Genesis 9:6).

Because He created everything, *God owns everything*. The earth is the Lord's. Those who "dwell therein" belong to God. He owns the cattle on a thousand hills. The silver and gold belong to Him. The church belongs to God. Civil governments belong to God. And of course children belong to God. But not only do children belong to God, their parents do as well. They claim sovereignty when in fact only God is sovereign. He is Lord of all. He is sovereign over all.

The devil was claiming sovereignty over the earth when he tempted Jesus in the wilderness. He showed Jesus "all the kingdoms of the world" (Matthew 4:8) and said, "All these things I will give You if You will fall down and worship me." (4:9) Jesus did not yield to Satan's lie. Our Lord knew that the devil was a usurper. The kingdoms of this world belong to God.

Yet Satan did have a legitimate claim over the earth as a steward. Adam had surrendered his title as God's lawfully appointed steward over the earth when he sinned against God by listening to Satan and following his advice. In order for God to reclaim this forfeited title to the stewardship of the earth, He sent His Son Jesus Christ to the earth to live a perfect life and reclaim title. (See the book on economics in the Biblical Blueprints series by Gary North, *Inherit the Earth*.)

Psalm 2 describes the kings and rulers of the earth in rebellion against God. But "He who sits in the heavens shall laugh." God has established His Son as king and God states, "I will give You the nations for Your inheritance, And the ends of the earth for Your possession" (Psalm 2:8).

Clearly, everything and everyone belongs to God. God has a special claim upon children because they are made in His image. God sent Christ to die on the cross for His people. He made a covenant with Abraham and with his children. "And I will establish My covenant between Me and you and your descendants after you in their generations, for an everlasting covenant, to be God to you and your descendants after you" (Genesis 17:7).

God gave circumcision as the sign of this covenantal relationship in the Old Testament. The New Testament sign of the covenant is baptism. In addition Jesus showed special interest in children when He said, "Suffer the children to come unto me, and forbid them not."

The State Has No Children!

The Bible tells us, "Behold, children are a heritage from the LORD, The fruit of the womb is His reward" (Psalm 127:3). God says to husbands, "Your wife shall be like a fruitful vine In the very heart of your house, Your children like olive plants All around your table" (Psalm 128:3). The government does not bear children. It can only adopt or control someone else's children. God brings children into the world through parents.

When I was in Israel several years ago, I had the opportunity to visit the site of the Qumran community where the Dead Sea Scrolls originated. The sect that lived there in ancient times was the Essenes. They did not believe in marriage and had no children of their own. The only way they could keep the sect going was by adopting children.

Those who worship the state as their god are like the Essenes. They want to claim all the children as their own. They are especially eager to have the children from Christian homes, so that they can indoctrinate them in the ways of secular humanism.

By the way, this is also the position facing homosexuals. They do not grow in numbers by reproduction. They grow only by recruiting. This a good reason why homosexuals should not be hired to teach. It is also a good reason for sending your sons to a Christian school.

So who owns the children?

God owns the children! The Bible answers that question clearly and emphatically. It is basic to the whole question of control.

Stewardship

But there is still a problem. I think I know what a Christian is going to say: "God owns my house, too." But you consider yourself the owner. The deed has your name on it. You pay the mortgage. You pay the taxes. Yes, you are willing to admit that in theory God owns everything, but in practice don't people own things?

Doesn't that apply also to children? We probably would not say we *own* our children, but we do say they are *our* children. I read about a father whose son had just scored against a rival sports team. "That's *my* son!" he proudly exclaimed to the lady sitting next to him. "He's *my* son, too!" she quickly reminded him. We want people to know that they are *our* kids — at least when they're behaving well and achieving something of value.

God tells the Israelite in Psalm 128:3 that "*your* children" shall be like olive plants round about "*your* table." We might infer from this that a man's children belong to him, just as his table can be said to be his. But that is not quite true. For instance, a father can't discard his children the way he might throw away a table. A father has responsibilities to his children because parents and children really belong to God.

Those who favor abortion argue that a woman has a "right to do what she wants to do with her own body." This argument ignores the fact that the unborn child is another person — God's person — so the mother has no God-granted right to destroy the innocent unborn. He will judge those who in any way promote abortion, for they are denying His sovereign ownership over people. The Christian should not accept the notion that a woman's body, or any person's body for that matter, belongs to that person. We belong to God, and we must live on God's terms. The child belongs to God. God in His infinite wisdom *entrusts* children to parents for their upbringing. The parents are to be faithful *trustees* under God. They are to be faithful stewards, caring for another Person's property. Everything we have belongs to God. Our land, houses, automobiles, talents, children, and everything else we call "ours" belongs to God. We are to use our material possessions to God's glory and to bring up our children "in the nurture and admonition of the Lord."

Humanistic Governments Claim They Own Everything

Civil governments that operate according to the religion of humanism claim ownership over children. They also claim to own everything else as well.

Consider the case of our income. The United States government claims that in principle 100% of our income belongs to it, since it also claims that in principle, the source of this income, property, belongs to it. This was not true prior to 1913. But with the passage of the income tax (assuming it really was passed legally), the federal government had all limits on its taxing powers removed.

The federal government does not actually tax 100% of our in-

come. If it did, everyone would quit working, and there wouldn't
be any income to tax. So the government exempts some income
from taxation. Then it taxes the remainder at a rate below 100%.
The top rates have in the past been over 90%, and currently are
50%. While it is encouraging to see the top rates coming down,
the fact remains that the government claims the right to tax all
income at 100%. (This is actually done in Sweden. Film producer
Ingmar Bergman fled Sweden in the 1970's when the government
taxed him 102% of his previous year's income.)

Consider private property. When we buy a house, we like to
think that we own it. The deeds I get for my property state that
my wife and I are *"tenants* in common" or *"tenants* by the entirety." I
always thought a tenant was a person who was renting from
someone else. Who is our landlord? You guessed it. The state lays
ultimate claim to our property. Just as the kings claimed that all
the land belonged to them in ancient times, so modern states
claim ownership over the land. As they claim the right to tax
100% of our incomes, so they claim the right to unlimited taxation
on our real estate.

The humanistic claim to ownership of land is seen in the story
of Tobiah and Sanballat. It is recorded in Nehemiah 5. The two
men had driven the people of Jerusalem to the brink of slavery
through confiscation, conscription, and abusive taxation.

Nehemiah, the godly governor of the province, confronted
their sin and exposed their power grasping schemes. The issue for
him was sovereignty. For that matter, the issue for Tobiah and
Sanballat was sovereignty, too. But *whose* sovereignty? For Nehemiah, God's sovereignty over the land precluded power plays. For
Tobiah and Sanballat, *their* sovereignty gave them absolute free
reign.

The humanistic state today, like the administration of Tobiah
and Sanballat, claims the right of "eminent domain." What it
wants, it takes. At least in the United States, the Constitution
provides that the taking is supposed to be for public uses, and
compensation is to be paid the landowner. But this is not always
honored in fact by the courts.

Recently, I received a letter from the Commonwealth of Virginia stating that they would be taking some of my property for highway purposes. At the same time, the county government is denying me the right to use this land for office buildings. Governments claim the right to our property through land use laws.

It is interesting that in the years 1912 and 1913, three major changes were made in the United States affecting property. The three changes were the Constitutional amendment providing for the income tax, the establishment of the Federal Reserve Bank, which regulates the value of our money, and the first zoning laws. (The Constitutional amendment authorizing direct election of U.S. Senators was also passed in 1913.)

All three of these changes grew out of a religious view which we today call humanism. All are based on the idea of state ownership of income, money, and land. When the *Communist Manifesto* was written by Karl Marx and Frederick Engels in 1848, they advocated centralized government control. They proposed centralized banking such as we have with the Federal Reserve Bank. They proposed the graduated income tax. They also called for all children to be educated in government-run schools.

Humanists are a minority in the United States today, but their program has been widely adopted. Are we surprised that a government that claims the right to all our income and all our property would also claim the right to our children? Of course the humanists want our children. No wonder they are fighting so fiercely to keep control! They want our children, and they want us to pay the tax bill. Christians have been putting up with this scheme since the 1830's. Why? Because they have forgotten the Bible's answer to the question: *Who is God's lawfully appointed trustee for the education of children, the state or the family?*

Worse: Christians, until very recently, seldom if ever self-consciously asked themselves this crucial question. But the humanists asked the question, and came up with the wrong answer: the state. Remember, the humanists' supreme principle, implicit or explicit, is *presently held power*. The only exceptions to this are revolutionary humanists, who respect future state power, and anarchists who call for the destruction of the state and who worship the power of the free market or the power of voluntary communes. Theirs is a power religion, just like the religions of the ancient pagan world. The state is the most powerful institution in the humanists' worldview, so it is their god. Public school teachers, not parents, are its lawfully appointed trustees.

Even though their answer was wrong, they got their way. They set the agenda for education. Their wrong answer was more powerful than no answer at all. Their answer won by default. This should remind us of the old political truth: "You can't fight something with nothing."

The Nature of the Fight

"For I am not ashamed of the Gospel of Christ, for it is the power of God to salvation for everyone who believes, for the Jew first and also for the Greek" (Romans 1:16).

Christian schools make no pretense of "neutrality." They are not ashamed of Jesus Christ, nor afraid to speak up for His cause. Jesus Christ is the Author and Finisher of our faith. He is the beginning and the end. He is the fountain of wisdom. He is the master teacher of all time. In Him are hid all the treasures of wisdom and of knowledge. He is the truth. He is the Saviour of the world. He is God. He is Lord over all.

The goal of the Christian school is clear. These schools exist to glorify God.

The Bible is the textbook for the Christian school. It is the only infallible Word of God. It is the basis for everything. All Scripture is inspired of God. "Inspired" means "God-breathed" (2 Timothy 3:16). Every word of the Bible is from God. We call this the *verbal* inspiration of the Bible. Ministers may err, churches may err, but God's Word is inerrant. It has no errors in it of any kind—no theological errors, no scientific errors, and no historical errors.

The Bible is the starting point and foundation for every area of knowledge. It is also the final court of intellectual appeal. The world about us is the creation of God. We can not understand that world apart from God. The believer and the non-believer may look out the window and say, "There is a cow eating grass." Both make the same statement, but each statement carries with it a different meaning. For the non-believer, the cow is a product of evolution in a chance universe; it is eating grass that has also evolved by chance. The cow has no particular purpose or meaning in the universe, except to serve mankind, which has no God over them. Man becomes the god of evolutionary forces.

For the believer, the cow is a God-created cow eating God-created grass. The cow is carrying out its purpose to provide dairy products and meat for man. This is for the purpose that man might glorify God. Man has God over him.

Everything has purpose and meaning in the universe because God gives it purpose. In Genesis chapter 1, we read that God created the sun and moon for a purpose—to rule over the day and over the night. Man was created to subdue the earth and have dominion over it. In this way he would glorify God. Man was to dress the garden and keep it. He was to be fruitful and multiply and fill up the earth. Jesus told His disciples to go into all the world and preach the gospel and teach all things that He had commanded.

Biblical Morality

Biblical morality involves living according to God's law. That law is summarized in the Ten Commandments.

In the Christian school there is no question about the standard of right and wrong. It is God's Word. The children are taught to worship God—not man, and surely not the state. The Bible forbids idol worship and the taking of God's name in vain. God's name is taken in vain every day in the public schools. The "name" of God includes His attributes and all the means whereby He makes Himself known to man. The "name" of God includes His Word and ordinances. To neglect the Bible is to take God's name in vain. The Bible is forbidden in the government schools.

God requires one day in seven as a day of rest. This teaches us that we are not saved by our works, but must look to God for salvation. The secular humanist believes that man is the captain of his soul and master of his fate. Man is his own saviour through the almighty state or the almighty something else—but never Almighty God.

Biblical morality teaches that the child is to honor his father and his mother. The Christian school is an extension of the home. Parents choose a school for their children and support that school. The school works closely with the parents to carry out the goals of the parents.

The government schools, on the other hand, undermine the authority of the parents by substituting the state and state-employed teachers in the parents' place. The school is not seen as a delegated agent of the parents, but as the delegated agent of the state. He who pays controls.

The Biblical prohibitions against murder, adultery, theft, false witness, and covetousness are daily taught in a Christian school.

The public schools have a problem. How can they speak out against theft? Certainly they cannot consistently oppose theft because it is contrary to God's Word. They can appeal only to expediency or the word of man. Since the government schools are funded with money taken from the taxpayers against their will and contrary to the Word of God, those schools have a real problem in opposing theft.

This is why free market economics is not being taught in government schools. A socialistic system can hardly teach free market economics. The state is buying the education it wants. It buys the attitude on the part of students that it wants. That attitude is one of obedience to the state.

Children are always quick to ask why they should do this or why they should not do that. What can the government schools say? "Do this because the majority of people think you should." Or: "Do that because I say so." They can only appeal to feeling, numbers, force, or something of that kind. The Christian teacher points to the Word of God. God is the ultimate authority.

The Effect of Christian Teachings

The Bible teaches that the child has inherited a sinful nature. He is born with this sin nature. The humanist believes the child is inherently good, or at least not inherently evil. Because the Christian knows his child is born with a sinful nature, he seeks the Biblical answer to sin. The Holy Spirit regenerates the sinner. The sinner turns to Christ in faith and repentance. This is the basis for sanctification as the child grows in the grace and knowledge of Christ. The goal is to be conformed to the image of the Son of God.

Thus, Christian education has a purpose. By the means which God has ordained, the Christian child is nurtured in the truth. The child is fed on the "sincere milk of the Word," and he can then grow toward maturity in the faith.

Life for the Christian has meaning because God gives life meaning. The Christian knows that he is to have dominion over the earth. He is called of God to subdue the earth (Genesis 1:27-28). Every area of life is to be studied in terms of God.

Suicide is a problem in the government schools because those schools have a pessimistic view of the future. For them, history is cyclical. Since there is no life beyond the grave, the secular humanist can only live for this world. Furthermore, the whole universe is seen as a giant grave. There is no escape. As the humanist cynic says, "Nobody gets out of life alive." The government schools are preoccupied with a gloom-and-doom outlook. They see problems, but not real solutions.

The Christian knows that history is linear, not cyclical. Time is a creation of God. Time moves toward the consummation of all things when Christ shall come to judge the living and the dead. The Christian has an optimistic view of the future because he knows that God controls the future.

The Christian knows the stone of Daniel 2 that becomes a great mountain which fills up the whole earth represents the kingdom of God. That kingdom will grow and prosper. Of the increase of Christ's government there will be no end (Isaiah 9). The kingdom will be like leaven which is hidden in three measures of meal until the whole is leavened (Matthew 13:33).

This same optimism characterized the pilgrims when they landed at Plymouth Rock in 1620. Because their religion was rooted and grounded in God, they were confident as they faced overwhelming difficulties in the new world.

As we look at the curriculum of the public schools in contrast with the Christian schools, we shall see more clearly the difference religion makes in education.

Public Schools Are Rival Religious Institutions

Whoever controls the education of our children will also determine the content of that education. If the state is in control, it will dictate what is taught. If parents are in control, their philosophy will be reflected in the curriculum.

Suppose the civil government were dominated by Christians. The schools under that government would then reflect the Christian philosophy of the civil rulers. We may be tempted to see this as the solution to the secular humanism in the schools.

"Let's get control of the government. Appoint or elect Christians to the public school board. Then make the curriculum reflect Christian values."

This plan will not work. It is not our job to recapture the public schools. They were never "ours" in the first place. In principle, they always belonged to the state, not to parents. He who pays the piper calls the tune. The state called the tune from the beginning. Parents are supposed to call the educational tunes.

We should work to develop a consistently Biblical basis for civil government. God is to rule in this area as in all areas of life. We should strive to elect righteous persons to public office. However, this is not the solution for the problem of what is taught in the schools. It is not the answer for the short term or the long term. Our goal should be to attain *Biblical ends* by *Biblical means*. Education is to be controlled by the parents. Parents are to see that the content is Biblical. Fathers are to bring up their children in the "nurture and admonition *of the Lord*." The children are to be taught the Bible. The Bible teaches that parents, not civil government, are responsible for education. So our goal is to have both Biblical content and Biblical control.

We could spend the next 25 years trying to wrest control of the public schools from the humanists. Meanwhile, our own children will be taught humanism if they go to the state schools. We must see that they get a God-centered education *now*. If Christian parents will act now, and *pay* now, they can have Christian education. It is a realistic goal. Taking over the whole governmental structure in the country will take much longer.

In the next chapters I want to show how the humanists are working to control our children.

Summary

Neither the family nor the state owns children. God is totally sovereign over all history. He is the Creator. Therefore, He owns everything.

Nevertheless, He delegates limited sovereignty to human institutions. Which human institution has been granted primary control over children, the state or the family? The Bible teaches that it is the family, as the next chapters clearly demonstrate.

Are schools to be agents of the state or the family? The Biblical position follows from the initial starting point: families have *stewardship* over *children*, and therefore over schools. The humanists deny this. They deny God's sovereignty, they deny the creation view or origins, and they affirm the sovereignty of man. This means in practice the sovereignty of mankind's most powerful earthly institution, the state.

The battle between Christianity and humanism is going on in the debate over education. Christians and humanists have rival views of God, man, law, and time. Obviously, the schools are training places for such views. Thus, there can be no reconciliation between these views. All education is therefore ethical; there can be no ethically neutral education.

The public schools are built on a myth: the myth of neutrality. This is how they keep Christian views out of the classroom. But as this anti-Christian bias becomes more obvious to Christians, Christians figure out that the neutrality doctrine is a myth.

Thus, Christians must seek to build up Christian schools, and steadily replace taxpayer-financed education. We should get civil government out of the education business.

In summary:

1. Neither the state nor the family owns the children.
2. Both positions are humanistic (man-centered).
3. God owns the children.
4. Children (like all men) are made in God's image.
5. He delegates primary responsibility to the family to serve as the trustee for children (stewardship).
6. Humanistic governments claim that they own everything.
7. They claim the right to tax us at 100% of income.
8. They control real estate development.
9. A major escalation of government power took place in 1913 in the United States.
10. Humanist views of state-owned property are dominant in the United States.
11. The humanists' supreme principle is the sovereignty of *presently held* political power.
12. Revolutionaries argue for the sovereignty of future political power held by them, at which time presently held political power will become the supreme principle.
13. Christianity is not neutral.
14. Christian education is not neutral.
15. Nothing that man does is neutral.
16. The Bible is the starting point for all knowledge.
17. The Bible is the final court of appeal for all knowledge.
18. All purpose is God-given.
19. God's word is the standard of morality.
20. Christian schools are the legal extension of the families that send their children to them.
21. State schools are the legal extension of the political sovereign that controls them and finances them.
22. The public schools cannot legally (or easily) teach Biblical morality.
23. Meaning comes only from God.
24. Teenage suicide is to a large extent the product of a humanistic view of life: no God-given meaning or purpose.
25. Christianity is optimistic with respect to the future.
26. Public schools are rival religious institutions.
27. Our goal should not be to recapture the public schools for Christ, for by law and morality, they are inherently immoral, anti-family, and therefore anti-Christian.
28. Our institutional goal for education should be the abolition of taxpayer-funded education.

2

GOD-CENTERED EDUCATION

Hear, O Israel: The LORD our God, the LORD is one! You shall love the LORD your God with all your heart, with all your soul, and with all your might. And these words which I command you today shall be in your heart; you shall teach them diligently to your children, and shall talk of them when you sit in your house, when you walk by the way, when you lie down, and when you rise up (Deuteronomy 6:4-7).

And you, fathers, do not provoke your children to wrath, but bring them up in the training and admonition of the Lord (Ephesians 6:4).

Some believers call themselves "New Testament Christians." The implication is that the Old Testament is not relevant to our day. (Fortunately, this belief is beginning to fade.) I have quoted above from both the Old Testament and the New Testament. Both Testaments teach that parents have the responsibility to educate their children. This is the point I want to make. I want to show how this makes a tremendous difference in the classroom.

It is a serious error to say that the Old Testament is not applicable to our day. When Jesus said of His Father, "Your word is truth" (John 17:17), He was referring specifically to the Old Testament. When Paul wrote to Timothy, "All Scripture is given by inspiration of God" (2 Timothy 3:16), bear in mind that some of the New Testament was not yet written. When the Berean Christians "searched the Scriptures daily" to check up on the preaching of Paul and Silas (Acts 17:11), it was the Old Testament that they were searching.

The passage quoted above from Deuteronomy 6 is the most

important one in the Bible in establishing the principles of Christian education. Jews call it the Shema (taken from the Hebrew word for "hear" with which the passage begins). Every Israelite was familiar with this passage.

The two most basic principles of education are taught in these verses. All the books on education ever written in the history of the world are not worth what we learn from these four verses. All the lectures on education ever given in the most esteemed universities of the world cannot equal the wisdom they contain.

The two principles are:

1. EDUCATION IS TO BE *GOD*-CENTERED.
2. EDUCATION IS A *PARENTAL* RESPONSIBILITY.

The thesis of this book depends on the truth of both principles: (1) the absolute sovereignty of God, and (2) God's delegated sovereignty to parents. The first principle is assumed throughout the book. I cover the first principle of education here; I cover the second in chapter three.

Who Is the God of the Public Schools?

The government schools are not God-centered. If you are a teacher in the government schools, and you mention the name of God (unless you are cursing), you will find yourself in a heap of trouble. A Christian who taught in the Maryland public schools told me that he was ordered to get a Bible off his desk and not to bring it back to school.

The only god allowed in the government schools is man. The state is also looked upon as god. The true and living God has no place in the public schools, either by design or by federal law. Kids aren't allowed to pray in the government schools. Oh, yes, I know. They can say a silent prayer. Even the Soviets haven't figured out how to keep people from praying silently.

Prayer

Several years ago, W. T. Woodson High School (located in Fairfax County, Virginia, not far from Washington D.C.) had a plaque on the wall of the student cafeteria. It contained a prayer that the students could voluntarily and silently pray before lunch. It was one of these generally worded prayers that did not mention Christ by name—nothing so offensive as that. Nevertheless, the plaque (put there by the students) had to be removed by edict from the powers that be. The reason given was that the plaque was hanging on the wall, and the wall belongs to the government.

The government still has military chaplains. The U.S. Senate still has a chaplain who prays brief, bland prayers before the sessions open. The House of Representatives has a meditation room. One member told me there was no way the Supreme Court would take it away.

The kids can't pray though. Why not? Because these are their formative years. The secular humanists who control the government do not want children praying to God when they are growing up. They might take God seriously. Does this sound like the Soviet system where children are not allowed by the government to attend Sunday School while they are growing up? (Yes, Virginia, it does.)

God Is Excluded

Is the education prescribed in the government schools God-centered? Hardly. Far from being in the center, God is not to be found even on the periphery. You couldn't find Him in the janitor's closet, let alone in the principal's office or in some classroom.

Yes, I know God is everywhere. He owns the cattle on a thousand hills. He certainly owns those public school buildings. But God isn't honored there. He isn't worshipped there. The government school teachers aren't assisting the parents in bringing up their children "in the nurture and admonition of the Lord." The government schools are feeding the children the husks of humanism. The real food is down the street at the Christian school.

What's on the Menu?

The public schools in our area publish the school lunch menu in the local newspapers. It's nice to know your kids are getting hot dogs at noon, so they don't get hot dogs again at the evening meal.

It's a nice gesture for working moms. Public schools aren't all bad.

What about the classroom menu? What's being served up there? You can be sure they aren't serving the same educational menu that you give your kids at home (if you have any time left for the kids after a busy day at the office). It won't be the same menu the pastor and Sunday School teacher provide on the Lord's Day, either.

This is the food you really ought to be concerned about. Who really cares if the kid gets chicken at school and again at home? Your chicken is better than that cafeteria stuff anyway. What the school is dumping on the plates at noon is not what education is all about. What are they dumping into your child's mind? I can tell you: it is garbage. It is humanistic garbage, and it is harmful to your child's spiritual health, his mental health, and his physical health.

Humanistic Lies

The fear of the LORD is the beginning of knowledge (Proverbs 1:7). Jesus said, "I am the way, the truth, and the life" (John 14:6). The only truth is God's truth. If we do not worship Jesus, then we can not attain unto truth. If we do not fear the Lord, we will not find wisdom. Jesus said that the devil is the father of lies. Humanists deny Christ. Here are some of the lies commonly taught in the public schools of America.

Lie Number One: God Is Irrelevant

This is the Big Lie. The Big Lie of humanism is that God is irrelevant, that is, God is not important to anything that is important. After all, how can God be important if He is left out of the education of our children? By ignoring God all day long in the textbooks and the teaching, the public schools are saying that God is not important. This is certainly not in keeping with the Biblical requirement that God be at the *center* of education.

Parents are to teach God's words diligently to their children when they are walking by the way, or sitting in the house, or when lying down or rising up (Deuteronomy 6:6-7). The idea is that

God permeates every aspect of the children's existence.

When they get on the government bus to ride to school, the children find that suddenly God is irrelevant. After all, school is a major part of a child's life. He spends most of his waking hours in school. His father (and often mother, too) goes off to work. He goes off to school. He makes friends at school. Most of his social activities probably center around the school. At school, God is ignored. God must not be important. He is only important on Sunday morning or maybe Wednesday night. God doesn't have anything to do with history, geography, math, art, music, or anything else that goes on in the world. That is the **BIG LIE**.

In God-centered education God is worshipped. He is not only important, He is more important than anyone or anything. He is at the center of all learning. His Word is a light and a lamp. The teacher acknowledges that the entrance of God's Word gives understanding. This is the **REAL TRUTH** to counter the Big Lie.

Lie Number Two: Man Evolved

The government schools teach that man evolved from lower forms of life. This is known as evolution. There is no place for a Creator God in the dogma of evolution.

The Bible teaches that God created the world out of nothing. Man was created in the image and likeness of God. Evolution is based on the idea of the creativity of chance. Evolution starts with the premise that matter is eternal. The Bible teaches that only God is eternal.

Creation is the opposite of evolution. That which evolved can not be created and that which is created could not evolve. To "evolve" means to develop out of something that already existed. "Create" means to make out of nothing.

The humanists who control the government schools are absolutely opposed to any teaching of creation in the public schools. There is a reason for their vicious opposition to the teaching of creation. If creation is taught, God is right back in the picture. If God created the world, then the world belongs to Him. God interprets the world. He has a purpose for the world and for man. God becomes the center of the universe. This is totally unacceptable for the humanists.

Creation is basic to God centered-education. Since God created the world, He is sovereign. He is Lord of all. He is Lord over the state, the church, and the family. The stamp of God is upon the created universe. There is no truth or understanding apart from Him.

Because God created man, man is called by God to have dominion over the earth. The humanist is interested in man having dominion over man rather than subduing the earth to God's glory.

Lie Number Three: Man Is His Own God

The humanists teach that man is god. This was the sin of Adam and Eve. Adam and Eve wanted to be as God, "knowing good and evil" (Genesis 3:5). Knowing good and evil means *determining* good and evil. In other words, Adam and Eve wanted to decide for themselves what is right and what is wrong, who is God, what is true, and so forth.

Under humanism, man is the source of law. In any philosophical system, the source of law is the god of the system. In humanism, man is the god of the system. What is right or wrong is decided by man — sometimes by the individual, and sometimes by a committee — not by the Bible. For example, the humanists who allow abortion say that a woman has the right "to do what she wants with her own body." Each person does what is right in his own eyes. There is no law originating from God. Man makes his own law.

A variation on this is that the majority decides what is right and what is wrong. Take a vote. If the majority decides that cannibalism is morally right, then that becomes the right thing.

Usually humanism degenerates into a totalitarian state, as took place in Nazi Germany under Adolph Hitler or as is the case today in Communist countries. A dictator determines right and wrong. It is all just another form of humanism — the idea that man is god and he determines good and evil.

God-centered education realizes that God is the source of all law, and that law is revealed by God in His Word, the Bible. The law of God is faithfully taught in the school. If God says something is right, then it is right. If God says something is evil, then it is evil. The Christian school delights in the law of the Lord.

Lie Number Four: The Child Is Inherently Good

This humanist lie is a denial of original sin. The Bible teaches that the sin of Adam is imputed (declared by God) to his descendants. Only Jesus Christ was not descended from Adam by ordinary generation and is without sin. Man's basic problem is his sin. God-centered education is based on the fact that the child has a sinful nature. Sin is dealt with in the child in terms of Biblical discipline. Basic to this is instructing the child to repent of sin and to trust in Jesus Christ as his Saviour.

The humanist denies original sin. For the humanist man's problem is his environment. Thus, the humanist wants to modify or change man's environment. When Adam was caught in sin, he blamed the woman. When God questioned the woman, she blamed the serpent. They were blaming their environment — the environment that God had given to them. Ultimately, they were blaming God. It was all His fault.

The humanist looks upon the child as an animal to be conditioned through the manipulation of his environment. Thus, humanist education becomes a *conditioning process*. Teachers are even called "change agents." Modification of behavior to suit humanist goals is important in humanist schools.

Because the humanist believes the environment is the problem, he denies individual and personal responsibility. The focus is on legislation to change man's environment. Thus, the use of the coercive power of the state is central in humanism.

God-centered education teaches personal responsibility for one's actions. God's grace is central in the Christian school. It is never mentioned in the government schools unless done in secret.

Lie Number Five: Man Saves Himself

Humanists deny the existence of God. Of course they do not believe in the Trinity. If there is to be any salvation, it must come from man. Liberal churches teach salvation by man's efforts rather than by the blood of Christ. That is why the liberal churches support public education. Humanism in the church finds an ally in the humanism of the government schools.

God-centered education teaches that Jesus Christ is man's only Saviour from sin. Salvation is by God's grace. Jesus Christ, the Son of God, died on the cross as a substitute in the sinner's stead. Through His atonement man is at peace with God. God is given all the Glory in salvation.

Lie Number Six: There Is No Hope for the Future

There was a time when humanistic education was positive. Humanists believed in the idea of inevitable progress. They had great hopes for the public school system. Some of them actually said that if everyone were given a free education, this would empty the jails. Horace Mann, called the "founder of the common school," put it this way in 1841:

> *The Common School is the greatest discovery ever made by man. . . .*
> Other social organizations are curative and remedial; this is a preventive and an antidote; they come to heal diseases and wounds; this is to make the physical and moral frame invulnerable to them. Let the Common School be expanded to its capabilities, let it be worked with the efficiency of which it is susceptible, and nine-tenths of the crimes in the penal code would become obsolete; the long catalogue of human ills would be abridged; men would walk more safely by day; every pillow would be more inviolable by night; property, life and character held by a stronger tenure; and rational hopes respecting the future brightened.

Well, the jails have never been more crowded. The streets have never been less safe. The lock business has never been better. And public school budgets have never been larger.

Today, humanistic education is increasingly negative. The older confident faith is fading. They are like people who are driving cars that have defective steering mechanisms. Their educational programs are producing students who fail—fail in school, and fail after graduation. Because humanists deny creation, the fall, God's law, and God's grace, they are not able to prepare children for the real world. The real world is the one that God created and governs. The real world has meaning and purpose.

Man-centered education produces students with data—"facts." These students do not know how to interpret this data correctly. They are without hope, and lack confidence in the future. The most common cause of death among young people in America (other than accidents) is suicide. Nancy Reagan is frequently seen on television pleading with young people not to take their own lives. Humanism depresses our young people. It offers only a gloomy outlook on life. Students turn to drugs, alcohol, and suicide. Humanism is boring.

A popular movie in the summer of 1986 was "Ferris Bueller's Day Off." It is a story of a high school senior who plays hookey for a day. The scenes of the classrooms in his public high school are hilarious. Teachers drone on and on. They ask the students questions. Silence. Then they answer their own questions. Students are staring blankly, glassy-eyed. One student is asleep with his head on his desk. The message is clear: public education is boring, useless, a waste of time. The audiences howled with laughter. The inmates and former inmates recognized their prison.

God-centered education has the opposite result. God created the world and man for a purpose. Man is to have dominion over the earth. He is to occupy (take over) the earth until Christ returns. Man is to proclaim the gospel to the whole world. History does not go around in cycles. It is moving toward the end, a glorious end in which Christ will come to judge the world.

Humanism Is Not the Answer

The Christian cannot in good conscience send his child to a school in which humanism is taught. Many private schools are humanistic. Humanism can be found in schools that call themselves Christian. But the public schools of American, run by the government, are shot through with humanism. Humanism is the new established religion in America. The public schools have become the new established church. The teachers have become the priests and priestesses of this new religion.

Summary

The public schools are a battle zone, figuratively and sometimes literally. The war is between two rival views of God. The source of the law of any system is its god. In humanism, that god is man.

The Bible teaches that God is God, and He has revealed Himself in the Bible. We begin with God and His Word, and we end with God and His Word. In humanism, we begin with man and his word, and end with man and his word.

The big lie of the public schools is that the God of the Bible is irrelevant. The textbooks never mention Him. Everyone assumes that children do not need to know anything about God, God's law, and God's Word in order to become educated people. This is Satan's own lie.

The Christian school must offer a better view of education. It must place God at the center of everything. God's Word is the standard, not man's word. Children must not be taught that man can know anything he wants without reference to God. Man can know nothing truly without reference to the God of the Bible.

In Summary:

1. The Bible teaches that parents must instruct their children in God's commandments.
2. Education must be God-centered.
3. Parents are in charge of education.
4. Government schools are not God-centered.
5. The god of the public schools is man.
6. Children are not allowed to pray publicly in these schools.
7. God is excluded on campus.
8. Christians need to read the "classroom menu."
9. The government schools are based on lies.
10. Lie one: God is irrelevant.
11. Lie two: mankind evolved.
12. Lie three: man is his own god.
13. Lie four: the child is inherently good.
14. Lie five: man saves himself.
15. Lie six: there is no hope for the future.
16. Humanism is not the answer.

3

PARENTS IN THE DRIVER'S SEAT

Hear, O Israel: The LORD our God, the LORD is one! You shall love the LORD your God with all your heart, with all your soul, and with all your might. And these words which I command you today shall be in your heart; you shall teach them diligently to your children, and shall talk of them when you sit in your house, when you walk by the way, when you lie down, and when you rise up (Deuteronomy 6:4-7).

And you, fathers, do not provoke your children to wrath, but bring them up in the training and admonition of the Lord (Ephesians 6:4).

In this chapter, I discuss the second principle of formal education: the parents' responsibility for the education of their children. We must begin our discussion with a consideration of the Biblical covenant. The covenants of the Bible all have the same five points:

1. A sovereign Creator God who runs everything
2. A hierarchy of authority with God at the top
3. A system of law (ethical rules) for dominion
4. A judicial system for making evaluations
5. A program for inheritance

In the Bible, each of the covenantal institutions will be governed by this five-point structure. The family is one of these institutions.

God in His wisdom and love has established three covenantal (oath-bound) institutions: the family, the church, and the state (or civil government). They are separate institutions. Any attempt by the authorities in one of these institutions to take control over the

35

other, except in specific Biblical instances of legal failure on the part of the leaders of the other one, is an infringement on the God-ordained sovereignty of the threatened institution. It is a violation of liberty.

Family Responsibility

In the beginning God brought Eve to Adam. They became one flesh. They established the first family. Any nation that weakens the family or tries to destroy the family is doomed. As goes the family, so goes the church. As goes the family, so goes the nation.

Education is the prerogative of the family, not the state. The *parents* are to teach God's words "diligently" unto *their* children. The state has no children. The father is the head of the family. Specifically, the father is commanded by God to bring up his children in the nurture and admonition of the Lord. "Nurture" refers to *instruction*. Notice that both principles from the Old Testament are repeated by Paul in Ephesians. It is the parents who have the responsibility to educate their children. That education is to be "of the Lord."

Parents have responsibility for the complete care of their children. This should begin before birth. Mothers should eat properly and should not use any harmful substances that would injure their babies. The Biblical approach is just the opposite of the abortion mentality that would destroy the unborn child.

The father assists the mother in preparing for the baby's birth. He is the breadwinner. He works at his calling to provide for his family. He gives her stability and support, in every sense.

The father and mother together provide love for their children from the beginning of life. This love and caring never ends. Thus, the welfare of children is a family matter. The child is provided shelter, food, clothing, medical care, religious training, and education.

A Blind Spot

Most Christians oppose the idea that the civil government should provide housing, food, clothing, etc. We say we do not believe in the "welfare state." We are opposed to socialism. We do not want a communistic system as they have in the Soviet Union.

While most Christians strongly oppose the idea that civil governments should provide cradle-to-grave security, many of them are blind on the matter of education. Somehow, we don't even question the idea of a public school system. We don't think of ourselves as being "on welfare" when we send our kids down to the neighborhood school. We need to think about this. Socialized education is no different in principle from socialized medicine or socialized anything else. When we send the children to the government school, we are accepting tax-financed welfare.

It is not necessarily wrong to accept a gift. That is to say, there is a place for charity in the Biblical scheme of things. Our churches carry on a diaconal ministry. As individuals, we may (and should) help a friend or neighbor in need. We have all kinds of voluntary associations to assist the needy. We give and we receive.

This is not the same situation as the public school. The public school system is not based on charity. It is not based on the principle of voluntarism. The public schools are funded with taxes. When we enroll our children in a public school, we are stealing from our neighbors.

Yes, that is what I said, and that is what I meant. Bastiat, the famous French writer of the 19th century, called it "legal plunder." The fact that plunder is legal does not make it moral.

The Christian then should take care of the education of his own children. He should not use force against his neighbor to rob his neighbor of his wealth, yet this is exactly what takes place with a public school system. The government is engaged in the redistribution of wealth.

Karl Marx advocated public schools in *The Communist Manifesto* (1848). His goal was to destroy Christianity by destroying the family. To destroy the family, he knew it would be necessary to destroy private property. Thus, the tax system was to be used to take property away from one person and give it to another.

The Bible teaches that taxes are to be paid for legitimate functions of government. Taxes are not to be paid to the government for the purpose of giving the property of one person to another person.

The responsibility to educate children belongs to the parents. They are to carry out this task from the time the child is born. The parents are to teach God's words diligently to their children. They are to teach while sitting, walking, when lying down, and when getting up. The idea is that *education takes place all the time and in every place*. The notion that education can only take place in some formal setting such as a school classroom is not a Biblical idea.

How Children Learn

There is a hierarchy in education. God is on top (point one: the sovereignty of God). God delegates the responsibility for education to parents (point two: hierarchy). Parents must determine what the children will be taught (point three: law), and they will judge whether the child is advancing (point four: judgment). They do this in order to transfer a heritage and inheritance to their children (point five: inheritance). The family must honor this five-point structure of the covenant in the field of education.

Children learn by example. I have noticed that subtle mannerisms of parents are seen in their children. I see them in my own children. When I call on the phone to a friend, I am often unable to tell whether I am talking to the father or his son, the mother or her daughter.

Children learn a great deal before they ever go to school. When the child is born, he cannot speak a word. The mother and father patiently teach the child their native language, and most of this teaching is by example. The child "picks up" the parents' language in the way he picks up anything else left within his reach.

Soon even a small child is able to speak fluently. Recently, I took Dorothy, one of my granddaughters, to McDonald's. On the way, she began to rattle off the books of the Old Testament. She is barely four years old. I couldn't name the books of the Old Testament after four years of college and four years of seminary. It wasn't because I was stupid; it was because God in His grace enables young minds to memorize astounding quantities of information, but this skill diminishes over time. (Anyway, I think so. I read about it somewhere. I forget just where.) Think of how they can sing advertising jingles that they hear on television — the same way older folks can remember radio jingles for products long gone, even if they can't memorize the books of the Bible very easily.

Dorothy said her daddy has been teaching her the books of the Bible on the way to school. Little children can learn far more than we realize, and they seem to be able to do it with minimum effort. The key is parental involvement.

But understand: a child does not intuitively learn the names and order of the books of the Bible. Parents have to help. Memorization of important material is a discipline. It is part of a structured program of teaching. The child does not learn this way on his own. He does not learn it on a field trip or in some sort of improvised "social action" project for four-year-olds. His parents work with him, and discipline him to learn the material.

Home Schooling

One of the most significant movements in education today is the home school. It is almost entirely confined to the Christian community. It is part of two trends, the general trend toward decentralization and the trend of Christians toward setting up alternatives to humanist institutions. Both trends are creating trouble for humanist educators.

John Naisbitt, in his book *Megatrends*, points out that decentralization is taking place in many areas of our lives. In education, he cites home schooling as an example. No doubt there is a reaction against centralizing education. We have seen the movement away from locally controlled small schools to the large consolidated school districts. A cabinet level Department of Education has been established at the Federal level. The home school can be seen as a wholesome movement in the other direction.

A far more important reason for the home school movement is the desire on the part of parents to have a direct hand in the education of their offspring. There are tens of thousands of children being taught at home in America today. We don't know how many there are in these home schools. This is a good thing; neither do the humanist planners. In some cases, the parents teach their own children. In other cases, two or more families cooperate in the task.

What are we to think of home schools? I applaud them. There are some Christian schools that oppose home schooling. Maybe they don't want the competition. I don't know. I think Christian schools should encourage home schools in every way. They should work with home schoolers instead of against them.

The Christian Liberty Academy in Illinois has a very large home school program. The number of children in the home schools is far greater than those enrolled in the regular academy. (The Christian Liberty Academy also has the largest Christian school physical facility in the country; they bought it from the public schools in 1985 for $1.5 million, with the money they had made from selling home school materials.) There is no reason the two should not work together to accomplish the goal of Christian education.

The Christian school which I operate had its roots in a "home school" some 27 years ago. I was teaching in a private school. My wife was home with several small children. She wanted to teach the oldest two at home. One was three, the other was four. My wife invited several families in the neighborhood to send their children over for two and one-half hours each day to be instructed. One of the mothers watched our two year old at her house. The arrangement worked to everyone's advantage.

After leaving the private school where I taught, I started a small school in the basement of a house. We had six students initially. This expanded to 10 students at the end of the semester. That fall I opened Fairfax Christian School with 32 students, ranging from kindergarten through the eighth grade. My wife and I taught them all, including two of our own. We held classes in our home. We had two classrooms downstairs. We lived upstairs "over the shop." It was a neat arrangement.

The strength of the home school movement is the direct control exercised by parents. The course of study can be tailored to the specific needs of the child. The program is flexible. A great deal of learning can and does go on in this type of teaching situation. One of the best ways to learn is by teaching, and I am sure the parents learn a great deal right along with their children.

I need to stress at this point that there are rival views regarding home schools. In fact, some of these groups fight more over *when* a child should start his formal education than *what* he should be taught. I believe in the traditional Protestant view that children should be catechized at a very early age, and taught to read very early—at age four or five. They should be reading their Bibles at age six. They *can* do it, and they *should* do it. Deliberately to keep the Bible a closed book for young children when they can be taught to read it is simply sinful. Yet there is actually a small and highly vocal movement of Christian home schoolers who follow a system based on the idea that children not be formally taught to read and compute until age nine or ten, unless they ask to be taught these skills.

I totally reject the idea—an idea that has its roots in humanism (the Montessori and/or Mormon movement)—that parents should postpone giving their children formal, structured, highly disciplined instruction until the children are nine or ten years old, or even older. Children should learn very early that time is an irreplaceable resource, that it is limited, and that to please God, we have to get to work early and hard. They should learn to appreciate the power and results of *structured, disciplined work*. They should learn this by example, too. We parents need to be structured and disciplined in our habits.

Jesus instructed the priests in the temple when He was a child of twelve (Luke 2:41-47). He is the Biblical model, not some baptized version of humanism's "free-form education for the naturally innocent child" model.

The Division of Labor

Sometimes when I advocate that parents should be responsible for the education of their children, I have been told that this is not practical. Many persons think that the *only* way parents can be responsible is for every family to teach the children at home. That is not the case.

Parents are responsible to feed their children, but it does not follow that all parents must be farmers. Parents are to provide shelter, but they don't have to build the family house in order to fulfill their responsibility. Every parent will be involved to some extent in feeding the children. They will shop for the groceries, cook meals, etc. They do not have to grow the food personally.

Parents have a part in providing shelter. Choosing a house, calling a plumber or electrician when needed, and performing a host of other chores around a house are part of providing shelter. The point is that parental responsibility does not mean that parents personally do everything.

"Now Abel was a keeper of sheep, but Cain was a tiller of the ground" (Genesis 4:2).

An important economic principle is seen in the first family that lived on earth. Cain and Abel had different occupations. This is the principle of the division of labor. Further on in this chapter of Genesis, we read about those who kept cattle, who handled harps and organs, and who worked with brass and iron. In the New Testament, Paul speaks in Romans 12 and 1 Corinthians 12 of the differing gifts that God gives to each of us.

Each person on earth is a unique creation by God. No two persons have the same set of fingerprints. We are different from every other person who ever lived on the earth. Biochemist Roger Williams wrote a book entitled *You Are Extraordinary*. In it, he shows that each person is biologically unique. This applies not only to fingerprints, but to other parts of our bodies.

God created us in His own image, and commanded us to have dominion over the earth. Man is able to think, to invent, to innovate. A robin today builds her nest the same way she did 20 years ago, or 200 years ago for that matter. Man thinks about his house and develops better ways to build.

Some people are skilled in music, some are better suited to be doctors, plumbers, engineers, or whatever. Some are given *the gift of teaching*. That is their calling from God. It is this principle of division of labor that improves living standards for everyone.

Each person pursues his own calling from God, and does that

kind of work he is best suited to do. We labor to have dominion in our area. Then we trade with one another so that the surplus we produce can be used to obtain things that will improve our lives. This trading is normally done through a medium of exchange which we call "money." (For details about how this system works, see Gary North's book, *Honest Money*, in the Biblical Blueprints Series.)

Division of labor occurs in a geographical sense also. Some parts of the earth are better suited than others for growing wheat, cotton, corn, or bananas. Crops are grown and goods are manufactured in those areas where they can be most efficiently grown or produced. Then we trade with one another, and everyone benefits.

God wants us to do this freely and peaceably. Then the dominion mandate can be best carried out. We subdue the earth and see improvement in our culture. When governments set up barriers to trade, the result is lower standards of living and conflict among men. Goods and services become more costly.

The division of labor applies in education. When governments place roadblocks in the way through compulsory attendance laws, taxation to redistribute wealth, zoning restrictions, and other regulations, they raise the cost of education. They also harm the quality of education. There is no longer the freedom for parents to exchange the fruit of their labor with one another. Free enterprise is superior to socialism. This is true whether we are talking about growing a crop, assembling a car, or educating a child.

Home schooling has its advantages. The parent takes direct control of his child's education. Home schooling also has its limitations. Especially as children get older, they need the benefits that come from division of labor. I have taught children in school, ranging from age four through high school. I have taught most of the subjects. Although I have four years of college and five years of graduate school, I cannot teach every subject well. I would not be a good music teacher. I appreciate good music, but I cannot find Middle C on a piano.

Would it be wrong for me to hire a tutor to teach my child music? I cannot imagine any Christian saying that it is immoral.

What if I hire a tutor to teach several of my children music? Still not immoral? What if a neighbor asks if he can help share the costs of the tutor, and send his children? The moment anyone says that this is valid, he has abandoned the principle of home schooling. But to defend home schooling as the only way, he must accuse the parents of doing something immoral.

The Christian school is simply a way that tutors take advantage of the division of labor. They have numerous parents send their children to them for instruction. They take advantage of something that economists call economies of scale. Several parents hire one tutor. They send the children to a central location for efficiency's sake. This is how poorer people take advantage of the tutorial principle. They pool their funds.

Those who defend home schools as the *only* Christian way to educate children are elitists. They are saying that only the children of parents who happen to be highly skilled teachers are to be given the best education. This is the inescapable implication of the "home schools only" outlook. The fact that its defenders refuse to admit this indicates that they either haven't thought through what they are saying, or else they are afraid to admit their elitism in public.

Several years ago, my wife and I were invited to Dallas to speak to a group of parents who were teaching their children at home. I observed two things on this trip. One was that the parents wanted to teach their children at home, but they were already seeking expert advice on how to do it. I also observed that they were making arrangements among themselves for social affairs (extra-curricular activities) for their children.

There is something else to consider. Word will get around the Christian community that one mother is especially skilled at teaching her own children. Other parents will eventually ask her to teach their children for a fee. The day she accepts this financial offer is the day home schooling has ended for her and the parents who send their children to her. Home schooling is therefore a temporary measure for the most gifted teachers. The division of labor principle works. Money talks. The most effective teachers will eventually abandon home schooling and become "headmasters" of Christian day schools.

The public schools have overdone the social end of things. They profess to teach "the whole child." There is no reason to turn the whole child over to any school. Even if the child is attending a Christian school, the school should not get involved in trying to do everything for the child. The parents can provide recreational and social contacts for their children.

The school should be seen as an extension of the home. It is not a replacement for the family. The school is not a separate institution any more than the factory, the grocery store, or the department store. The school is a place where the parent can get specialized help in the education of the child.

When should parents send the child to a Christian school? When the teaching staff of that school can impart more information and better work habits to the child for the same price, including the price of the parents' time. Parents eventually do this when the child reaches college age. Most parents do this a lot earlier.

Christians must not make a cult of home schooling. The cult mentality says: "Mine is the *only* way." Only if the Bible teaches that one way is the only way should we accept it as such. Given that the overall approach is moral—no compulsory tax financing of education, and no implicit theory of the innate innocence of the child—lots of ways are good. There is no single way that is best for every family.

Summary

God has delegated to parents the responsibility of educating their children. This education is to be comprehensive: moral, technical, economic, etc.

Parents may not legitimately delegate this financial responsibility to others without their consent. They are allowed to hire specialized tutors to assist them. A school is simply an extension of the family. Teachers are tutors who have used the division of labor to reduce costs by tutoring many children at once. A school is simply a development of the tutorial system. It is the way that less wealthy people can take advantage of the division of labor and the tutorial system.

We must be very wary of cult-like attitudes in Christian education, the view that "our way is the only way." There are many sorts of children, many sorts of skills, and many sorts of ways to impart skills to children. But eventually, they all involve discipline and structure.

In summary:

1. God assigns to parents the responsibility of instructing children.
2. The Bible is God's word.
3. Education is God-centered.
4. Education is the parents' responsibility.
5. Christians say they oppose the welfare state.
6. Yet Christians support the welfare state's education system.
7. When we send our children to a taxpayer-financed school, we are accepting tax-financed welfare.
8. Karl Marx recommended public education as a means to weaken family responsibility.
9. Children learn by example.
10. They learn a lot by watching parents.
11. Home schools take advantage of this aspect of children's learning processes.
12. Children should be receiving disciplined, structured education by age 5.
13. Parents should make use of the division of labor principle when educating their children.
14. In most cases, this involves sending children to a Christian school; the debate is over just when.
15. The answer is: When the parents no longer have the time and skills to compete with professional teachers in a local Christian school.
16. When a gifted home school teacher accepts her first pupil from outside her family, she is no longer involved in home schooling.
17. We should avoid cult-like attitudes regarding education.

4

HE WHO PAYS THE TEACHERS
WILL CONTROL EDUCATION

Then the king [Nebuchadnezzar] instructed Ashpenaz, the
master of his eunuchs, to bring some of the children of Israel and
some of the king's descendants and some of the nobles, young men
in whom there was no blemish, but good-looking, gifted in all wisdom, possessing knowledge and quick to understand, who had
ability to serve in the king's palace, and whom they might teach the
language and literature of the Chaldeans. And the king appointed
for them a daily provision of the king's delicacies and of the wine
which he drank, and three years of training for them, so that at the
end of that time they might serve before the king (Daniel 1:3-5).

Wow! A free education. Plus the delicacies of the king's table.
Social mixing with the sons of the rulers. Full-time tutors, too.
What an opportunity!

But what kind of opportunity was it? It was an opportunity to
serve the king. The expense of their education was not being provided as a free gift. There was a price to be paid. In the case of the
three young men, known by their Babylonian names of Shadrach,
Meshach, and Abednego, the price was a visit to the fiery furnace
(Daniel 3:8-30).

He who pays the piper calls the tune. The Bible says that God
is the source of all wealth (Deuteronomy 8:17), the source of all
good things (James 1:17). God pays all the pipers. We are His pipers. He calls the tune.

There is no such thing as a free education.

47

Organization

If you want to find out who is calling the institutional tune, find out who is paying the piper. In education, it isn't always clear just who is paying the piper. The less clear it is, the more power the hired pipers will possess.

As in the court of Nebuchadnezzar, education is delivered by tutors. The principle of sovereignty is always hierarchical. God delegates authority to men, and they in turn must delegate authority to those under them. Tutors possess authority over children only to the extent that they have been granted lawful authority by those who are financing the educational system. But if this control is not actively exercised by those who pay, then the tutors will be tempted to believe that they are sovereign, just as sinful man concludes that his own strength has made him wealthy (Deuteronomy 8:18). The servants will then begin to dictate terms to the sovereigns.

This is the age-old story of bureaucracy. In ancient Babylon, the king could say, "Off with their heads!" In the modern world, sovereigns can say, "Off with their funds!" If they are in any way prohibited from saying this, then the bureaucrats will steadily become the sovereigns in fact, if not in law.

He who pays the piper had better call the tunes, or else the pipers will start calling them, and then demand higher wages for fewer tunes.

Structuring the Christian School

Christian schools can be organized in several ways. The school can be under the authority of a church. Elders, deacons, bishops, or the congregation itself would have control in a church school. The church might have a school board to look after the policies and operation of the school. Parents would exercise control in various ways. They might be officers in the church, might have a vote in congregational meetings, and might serve on the board.

Another type of organization is a Christian school society made up of interested parents. The parents select a board which effectively runs the school. This affords the parents a considerable amount of control.

Yet a different arrangement is the profit-seeking, owner-operated private Christian school. I operate this kind of school, so am very familiar with it. We have a taxpaying school. The private Christian school which I operate has no board.

A closely held corporation could also run a school, either on a taxpaying or tax-exempt basis. Or the corporation could be publicly held.

Control Through Enrollment

How does a parent control the education of his child in these various forms of organization? The parent has the power of choice. He may choose among the various schools available in his community. If he doesn't like any of them, he has the option to educate his children at home, start another school, or move to another community.

The government school allows no choice. You are assigned a school district based on where you live. District lines may be redrawn at will. The school may be closed, and the children sent to another one. The government may bus your child across town. When I was in Louisville, Kentucky, several years ago, families told me that some of their children went to local schools, while others were bussed miles away in different directions. For the most part, the government dictates which school your child will attend.

Deciding to patronize one Christian school rather than another is the most important choice the parent makes. The parent is in control. In a free market economy, the consumer is king. Consumers make millions of choices in the marketplace every day. They choose this brand of soap rather than that one. They buy this make of car rather than another. They decide what they want to buy, how much they will pay, and from whom they will buy. They have the money, so they have control. If a seller says to a consumer, "Take it or leave it," the consumer can usually leave it. The seller gets no sale.

In being free to choose a school for his child, the parent is in the same situation. *Buying an education for a child is a free market transaction.* No coercion is used, nor should it be used. The parent is not forced to enroll his child in a school he does not like. He is not forced to pay for something he doesn't want.

Not only may the parent enroll his child in the school of his choice, but also he has the option to withdraw the child at any time. God has created man as a free moral agent. The father is given the freedom and responsibility to provide for the education of his children. Parental control of education is absolutely basic in the Biblical scheme of things.

Parental Control and Financing

A Supreme Court justice said that whatever the government subsidizes it may legally control. *Money talks.* It talks in politics, and it talks in the free market. It is the instrument of control.

The founding fathers of the United States realized that man is a sinner. They knew the danger of a powerful centralized government. They wrote into the United States Constitution a system of checks and balances to control the Federal government. Money could be spent only if appropriated by Congress. All tax bills must originate in the House of Representatives. It is the more numerous branch of the legislature. The term of office in this branch is only two years. A free spending House of Representatives must stand before the voters every twenty-four months, thus giving the people better control over government.

(That spending hasn't been restrained in recent decades for reasons that are beyond the scope of this book. In any event, the authors of the Constitution recognized the importance of the purse strings.)

Pocketbook control is important in a Christian school. If parents do not enroll their children in a school, the school will suffer financially. The material prosperity of a school is dependent on the willingness of parents to pay tuition.

Is this morally correct? Christians might ask:

Why should a Christian school be concerned about "material prosperity"? After all, the school is supposed to be doing the work of the Lord. A school is not a commercial enterprise. It is not concerned with the bottom line. Who cares whether it makes a profit or not?

This is the problem with a lot of our thinking. We tend to equate poverty with spirituality. We suppose that to be poor is to be godly. In Deuteronomy 28:1-14, God promises His people that if they obey His commandments, all kinds of blessings will come to them. Their fields, cattle, sheep, etc. will be blessed by God. These are material blessings. God gave them a land flowing with milk and honey. He increased Abraham's flocks and made him rich with silver and gold. He prospered Job because Job was obedient.

Jesus says that God's people are to inherit the earth. (Gary North's book on economic principles in the Biblical Blueprints Series is titled: *Inherit the Earth*.) God tells us in the Old Testament that when riches increase we are not to set our hearts upon them. Jesus warns of the danger of worshipping mammon instead of God.

We should not conclude that because worshipping material things is wrong, the material universe itself is sinful. Man is a sinner, and the curse is on the ground because of man's sin. God created the material universe for man to cultivate and enjoy. Man is to have dominion over the earth.

What does this have to do with pocketbook control over a Christian school? I think we need to answer that question by looking further at the reasons for educating our children.

Why Educate Our Children?

We teach our children the way of salvation. We teach them to love God and to serve Him. We want the school to assist us in helping our children to know God. God has called us to have dominion over the earth. Adam was to dress the garden and to keep it. Work is a basic institution. Man's labor is under the curse because of Adam's sin. Man must work to support his family. A tithe of the increase of his wealth is to be given to God. Some of his wealth is to be given to the poor.

A child learns to read in order that he may read the Bible for himself. He also needs to be able to read books, magazines, and newspapers. A person needs information in order to improve his standard of living. Reading is an important means of gaining knowledge. A Christian school that produces superior readers is providing a valuable service to the parents.

The same can be said about the study of numbers. Numbers represent relationships that exist in God's world. Arithmetic and mathematics are vital to an understanding of the world. The computer is an important tool in modern business. The advances in scientific technology could not have taken place without the study of mathematics. The study of physics, chemistry, biology, history, art, music, etc. all serve to enrich our lives.

Educating our children is an *investment*. It has a monetary benefit. When we choose a school for our children, we want to know how that school will help prepare our children for the future. We also equip him to support us in our old age, if this becomes necessary (Exodus 20:12). This is one reason why your child's tuition bill should not be regarded as part of the family's tithe. Tithes go to God; investments are made with after-tithe income.

The school that is excellent will be rewarded. Parents will determine which of several schools provides the best return on their educational dollars. The schools that do a poor job will be weeded out over time. The ones that operate most efficiently will expand. This is how pocketbook control works.

A few years ago a Presidential commission dealing with education in America reported that we have a "rising tide of mediocrity" in the public schools. This is exactly what we should have expected, and what critics of the public schools predicted a century ago. Parents have the greatest incentive to see to it that their children get a quality education. The government schools don't permit effective pocketbook control by the parents.

This system was deliberately designed by professional, state-hired educators to reduce parental control. Incompetent teachers are retained in the public schools because they have tenure. They are also protected by militant teacher unions with political power.

The schools are not competitive because there is a virtual government monopoly on education. The result is mediocrity or worse. The cost is much too high because the state schools are not answerable to the parents directly. They are funded by the taxpayers through the politicians.

Parental Control and Discipline

A major complaint about the public schools is the lack of discipline. Some teachers get extra pay for "combat duty" in the inner cities. The situation is so bad that schools have had to bring in uniformed police to walk the halls. Murders occur at our government schools. Dope is peddled all over the place. Physical attacks on the teachers are a problem, not to mention the verbal abuse the teachers are subject to.

Why is discipline a problem in the government schools? I was once asked to speak to a public school PTA (Parent-Teacher Association) on the subject of discipline. I warned them at the time of the invitation that I was opposed to the public school concept. They said to come anyway because they were getting "desperate" and needed advice. I took my Bible and gave them both barrels. I pointed out that the secular basis on which government schools were operating was their problem. You can't remove God and the Bible from the schools and expect to maintain order. The students cannot be told that they have an animal origin, and then be expected to behave as human beings.

The government schools have discipline problems because they have divorced education from God and from the family. The word "discipline" is from the Latin word for "disciple." A disciple is a learner. What we commonly call discipline should be termed punishment. Discipline has to do with learning. If there is a lot of teaching and learning going on in a classroom, there will not be a need for much punishment.

Learning has to be set in a moral and religious context. It involves a relationship to God and His world. The Christian school is teaching love for God and love for our neighbor. The Christian school teaches responsibility under God's law. Children respond to this. It is the loving care of a parent extended to the classroom by teachers who stand in the place of the parents.

The government school today has only force. The kids are forced to come, and taxpayers are forced to pay the bill. The teachers are controlled by the state, not by the parents. The teachers do not get cooperation from the parents because the parents have not freely chosen to place their children in the school. When a child misbehaves in a government school, what is the teacher supposed to do? The teacher can not appeal to the authority of God or His Word. This is not allowed in our secularized government schools. The schools have difficulty suspending or expelling the children. That goes contrary to the statist philosophy of compulsory education. They compel the children to attend school. It is difficult to turn around and compel the children to stay away.

The teacher in the government school tries to get parental cooperation with an unruly child. Many of the problem children in the schools come from homes in which the parents don't care anyway. That is often the source of the problem. The homes are often without a father. This situation itself is frequently caused by the welfare state with its anti-family policies. So the teacher gets little or no cooperation from the parents.

The situation in the Christian school is different. The parents place their children in the school voluntarily. The children are accepted by the school in a free market transaction. The parents are paying the tuition. They won't stand for disruptive classrooms that cheat their children out of the education they are paying for with hard-earned money. They know that there is no such thing as a free lunch, and there is no such thing as free education. Because they are paying directly for the school, they have much greater interest in a good atmosphere for learning.

In short, money talks.

Children misbehave in Christian schools also. Children are born with sinful natures, and perfection is not reached on this earth even by the most sanctified. The difference in the Christian school is that through the regeneration of the Holy Spirit, the child receives a new nature. The law of God can be freely taught.

The teachers counsel and pray with the students in terms of God and His requirements.

The parents support the teachers in a Christian school because *the school is both religiously and financially an extension of the home*. I remember the last day of school in my first year of teaching at our Christian school. One of the eighth grade students decided that she was going to do whatever she pleased that day. I asked whether she had work to do, and when she replied in the negative, I gave her an assignment. "I'm not going to do it!" she defiantly replied. I said nothing. I walked to a corner of the room and called her father on the telephone. He asked that she come to the phone. He told her to do the assignment. When she came back she assured me she would do the work, but "only because my dad said to." "That is fine with me," I retorted, "because I'm only working for your father anyway."

The Christian school has the correct foundation for orderly learning. If a student does not obey in the classroom, the matter can be referred to the parents. If the parents exert Biblical authority, good results should be forthcoming. If the parents do not want to support Biblical behavior in the school, the school can expel an unruly student. If the school does not maintain standards, then the parent can enroll the child in a school that does.

Another factor that makes for good order in the Christian school is that Christians worship a God who has created a world with purpose. God states in Genesis 1:16 that he made the sun to "rule the day" and the moon to "rule the night." This indicates *purpose* in the universe. Everything in God's universe has purpose and meaning. All history has meaning because God is the author of history. We do not live in a chance universe.

The Christian school classroom reflects order and meaning because the Christian seeks to pattern his thoughts after God's thoughts. The secular classroom reflects the chaos and disorder that stem from a denial of creation. When God is left out, learning has no meaning. Any "discipline" in such a school becomes mere imposition of force.

Parental Control and Academic Results

Two decades ago, a Japanese student was attending Westminster Theological Seminary in Philadelphia. He wanted to attend a major American university the following year. He had to take the Graduate Record Exam as a requirement to get in. It had both an English section and a mathematics section. He had not had a course in mathematics since high school, at least six years earlier. He took the exam. Afterward, he complained to one of his classmates: "The mathematics section was too easy. Too easy." He shook his head in disbelief. This was for *graduate* students. When the results came in, he was in the 80th percentile in English, but the 99th percentile in mathematics. He was correct; the exam was too easy.

Several years ago, a math examination was conducted among the major nations of the world. The Japanese, with a 41-1 pupil-teacher ratio, did the best. Two things characterized the Japanese approach. They had drill-drill-drill in the elementary schools. Also, the parents taught the children before they entered school.

Both ideas have been anathema in American public schools. Drill is considered a bad word. It is considered dull. Parents are discouraged from teaching their children at home. Years ago, we enrolled a first grader whose father was with the United States Department of Education (or whatever it was called then). The father had a Ph.D. The first grader could not even count to 10. I thought he must be a "slow learner." I soon discovered that he had an excellent mind. The parents had deliberately refrained from teaching the boy. The result was that other students were well ahead of him.

Government school officials don't want much parental involvement. They want the parents in their capacity as taxpayers to pay the bills. They want the children fed, clothed, and put on the bus. They want them to attend PTA to make it look as though they have some say in the education of the children. What they *don't* want is parents who try to "dictate" to the school about such things as textbooks and discipline. Many school systems not only give no homework, but even forbid the children to take the text-books home. The result is that parents in government schools have little or no involvement in the education of their offspring.

If parents are concerned about the poor academic results in the public schools, they have a difficult time making the necessary changes to improve the schools. Since the schools are public, they must be "democratic" in the sense that everyone must be treated equally. I will go into more detail in a later chapter. I will only point out now that academic standards in America's public schools have dropped dramatically.

The schools just tell the parents to give them more money and everything will be fine. The schools don't give the parents control, but they like to hold the parents responsible for the poor academic results.

Deflecting Parental Control: Politics

Parents have very little say in the way public schools are run because *the real control is political*. Even the political control can be rather remote. The City of Fairfax is a political entity surrounded by Fairfax County, Virginia. Children in Fairfax City attend public schools which are supervised by a school board. That school board is appointed by a City Council which is elected by the citizens. The schools in Fairfax City are not even run by the city school board. They are operated by the Fairfax County School Board which is appointed by the County Supervisors, who are elected by residents of Fairfax County. Added to this situation is the fact that the State Board of Education (appointed by the Governor) has a lot of say in the local schools. This is not to mention the State Legislature, the Congress, the Federal Department of Education, plus all the courts up to and including the Supreme Court!

Who is in charge anyway? Certainly not the parents. Maybe a case could be made that the NEA teachers union controls the schools. They are the most powerful political lobby in the country. They want to be the foxes who guard the henhouse. They want the parents to subsidize the humanists' indoctrinating of their children. They vote as a bloc to get what they want.

The teacher-training institutions also exercise important influence. That is why the humanists want their graduates to have a monopoly on the public school pulpits. The courts exercise tremendous influence, virtually dictating school policy in some areas.

The little red school house with your friendly neighbors setting policy is long gone in America. (So, increasingly, are friendly neighbors. Do you know the names of the family members of the people who live in the houses four doors on each side of you? How many times have you eaten dinner with them?)

In short, humanist kidnappers are demanding ransom, and Christian parents are paying it. But they never send the children back. They keep them, and then try to get the parents to send them on for "advanced kidnapping": a humanistic college.

Buying Control

When you enroll your child in a Christian school, the situation is different. You can directly influence and control the education of your child. In the Christian school I operate everyone knows that "Mr. T" is the headmaster. If there is a question about curriculum, transportation, discipline, report cards, or whatever, the parent knows who is responsible.

Earlier, I showed how parental control makes for good discipline. The same is true for academics. The parent in effect says, "Produce, or I will place my child in another school." He looks for results, not excuses. That huge playing field at your local public high school is an excuse. "Look at our terrific facilities. How can you complain?" The issue isn't a school's facilities; the issue is the quality of the education received and retained.

Parents don't have to worry about all the ingredients that go into making a school a good one. When I go to the grocery store, I do not concern myself with how they manage to give me such variety and quality for the money I pay. That is their problem. If they don't produce, I go elsewhere.

But suppose the government had a monopoly on groceries. Can you imagine what it would be like? I can. There would be high prices, inferior merchandise, short hours, and long lines.

There would be surly check-out girls. (You know what the slogan of most government bureaucrats is, if they have to meet the public? "Surly to bed, and surly to rise.")

The Christian school cannot afford poor academic quality. Parents are not forced to pay, and they will not continue to patronize the schools if they do not produce. The Christian school gets the message quickly if it is not producing.

In contrast, the government schools take years, even decades, to respond to needed educational change. Even then, because they are based on faulty premises, they flounder from one bad experiment after another. Christian schools have a long way to go, but they are already well ahead of the government schools, and the price is much lower.

Control and Change

The humanists are fond of saying, "We live in a changing world." They like to think of themselves as "progressive." Humanist education is called "progressive education." It should be called "regressive education" because it is a throwback to the kind of state-controlled system that characterized ancient Sparta in Greece. The system was ultra-conservative. No changes were allowed.

This is interesting because the secular humanists of our day think Christians are "reactionaries" who want to "turn the clock back." The fact of the matter is that Christians who think Biblically realize that history is linear. We are moving toward the consummation of all things. The Christian does not worship change, but he realizes that *progress comes with change*. Change in itself is not always good. "New management" may not be "better" management. Change may be for the worse as well as for the better. The Christian can determine whether change is for the better by judging all things by that One who never changes, God Himself.

Modern life moves along quickly in so many ways. Most of the jobs that exist today were unheard of 50 years ago. Anyone who does not keep pace with the modern world will find it more difficult to adjust. The point is that the schools must prepare children for the real world in which we live and the world which will exist in the future. The government schools are at a distinct disadvantage here because they cannot adjust quickly. They are a ponderous bureaucracy, not an efficiently run business. They are subject to the whims of politicians whose main concern is with the next election, not the next generation.

Parents who send their children to a Christian school have a much better way to see that the program of the school meets the needs of the children as the parents perceive them. The Christian school with its local control and parental involvement has the flexibility to make the changes that are needed to improve education.

Summary

The question of parental authority cannot be separated from the question of school financing. To the degree that parents are not totally responsible financially for the education of their children, to that extent they have abdicated control over that education. He who pays the piper calls the tune.

State education is deliberately designed to transfer the control over education away from parents, and especially Christian parents, and toward humanist control through politics and bureaucratic licensing. Teacher unions have become political, for this is the way the educators retain control over the schools.

Christian voters have repeatedly voted for this system. They have believed the lie: "free education." There is no such thing as free education.

It is the power of the purse that constitutes the parents' primary means of control over the content and method of education. To abdicate this financial and moral responsibility is to deliver the next generation into the hands of the kidnappers.

In summary:

1. God pays all pipers.
2. God calls all tunes.
3. There is no such thing as a free education.
4. The less clear it is who is paying the pipers, the more power the pipers have in calling the tunes.

5. The school is morally an extension of the family.

6. Teachers are hired tutors.

7. There are several ways to structure control in a Christian school.

8. Parents gain control over the schools by retaining the authority to buy their children an education at competing schools.

9. Government school systems restrict this freedom of choice.

10. Without a free market in education, the parents authority is restricted or even eliminated.

11. Money talks.

12. Too many Christians equate poverty with spirituality.

13. Educating our children is an investment.

14. Tuition payments are not part of a parent's tithe.

15. Discipline problems are rising in public schools because parents are not in control.

16. Learning must go on in a moral context.

17. The government school today uses force, not moral suasion.

18. Parents can buy better discipline in private schools.

19. Money talks.

20. Government school officials do not want parents to control them.

21. The real control is political.

22. Teacher unions are therefore political. The foxes wish to guard the henhouse.

23. Humanist kidnappers are demanding that Christian parents pay ransom, but the children are never returned to them.

24. Christians schools are forced to compete. They dare not ignore most parents.

25. "Progressive education" is regressive: it is ancient humanism.

26. Christian education is progressive: a philosophy of *linear history.*

27. Government-controlled schools are inflexible bureaucracies.

5

EDUCATION SHOULD BE VOLUNTARY

And Moses commanded them, saying: "At the end of every seven years, at the appointed time in the year of release, at the Feast of Tabernacles, when all Israel comes to appear before the LORD your God in the place which He chooses, you shall read this law before all Israel in their hearing. Gather the people together, men and women and little ones, and the stranger who is within your gates, that they may hear and that they may learn to fear the LORD your God and carefully observe all the words of this law, and that their children, who have not known it, may hear and learn to fear the LORD your God as long as you live in the land which you cross the Jordan to possess (Deuteronomy 31:10-13).

Several comments are in order. First, the law was to be read to all the residents in the land, believers and unbelievers, once every seven years. This public event was part of the *civil covenant* with God. God held each person accountable to observe His law, and He held the authorities accountable for its enforcement. Ignorance of the law was no excuse for breaking it, for no one in the land was to remain ignorant of God's law.

Second, because this event was to take place only once every seven years, strangers and unbelieving residents in Israel were not required to attend regular religious services in which they might hear the law. Only once in every seven years was the civil requirement imposed on them.

Third, this law was supposed to be in force only during the Old Testament era in which Israel remained in the promised land. Once they went into foreign lands, they could not be expected to enforce such a requirement.

Attendance at this occasional civil ceremony was required of all residents of the land, but it was a *civil* ceremony. While all the law was read, it was primarily a civil law function as far as it pertained to the unbelieving stranger within the gates (protection) of Israel.

Compulsory Church Attendance

Let me try out the following argument. See if you agree or disagree with it.

> "Nothing is more important on earth than to accept Jesus Christ as your Lord and Savior. Every person should have an opportunity to hear the Gospel of Christ. Therefore, the civil government should pass a law that requires each person to send his children to a Bible-believing church every Sunday until the child reaches the age of 16 years old. This will make them better-informed, God-fearing citizens, and therefore it will enable them to meet the requirements of well-informed citizenship in our nation."

Such arguments do not ring true in the ears of modern men. Yet for well over a thousand years, this line of argumentation would have appeared false, not because it requires people to attend church, but because of its suspicious weakness. Almost no Christian society in the Middle Ages would have exempted anyone over age 16 from attending church weekly. It was not just children who were required to attend; it was *everyone* except Jews, who were given a special exemption.

Why don't we believe these arguments any more? Many reasons. We see that this would involve the civil government in a positive fashion. The state would be requiring people to *do* something. Unless we are socialists, we see the state as an institution for *suppressing public evil*, not making men good. The state is supposed to be a *negative authority*, not a positive instrument of salvation.

We also see that such compulsory attendance laws would interfere with men's freedom to make up their own minds about God, and they would interfere with a family's legal immunity (right) from state interference in teaching their children the religion of the household. It is the parents' God-given responsibility to train their children, not the state's.

Irresponsible Parents?

But what about the following response?

> "But we know that some parents are irresponsible. They do not know God. They care nothing about God. They will teach their children a false view of God. They will not obey God and train their children in the admonition of the Lord. Thus, it is our responsibility as Christian citizens to compel these short-sighted parents to send their children to church."

Are there irresponsible parents? Of course. Will these parents refuse to send their children to church? Most certainly. Should their children hear the Gospel? Absolutely; God will hold both the parents and the children responsible on judgment day. But are these arguments a sufficient reason for taking the children away from the parents one day a week to indoctrinate them — that *is* the word — in a rival religion, even if the religion is Christianity? I don't think so, and I don't think you do, either.

But the humanists require Christians to send their children to state-licensed schools, five days a week, six hours a day, and then encourage the children to get involved in after-school extracurricular activities.

Let's ask another important series of questions. Are there parents who will not give their children religious instruction? No, there aren't. Every parent gives his children religious instruction. There is no neutrality. They may give them instruction in a religion other than Christianity. Maybe they will teach them Judaism, or Islam, or Buddhism. Maybe they will teach them alcoholism, or revolutionism, or debauchery. Maybe (probably) these days it will be humanism. But some world-and-life view will be taught in the home. There is no escape from a worldview. Men cannot think or act without one.

Therefore, any attempt on the part of the state to require a child to listen to Christian preaching once a week is an assault on the families of those who do not accept Christianity. Of necessity, such a law would be an attempt to impose a rival religion on the families of unbelievers. It is not simply a question of obeying civil laws that suppress public evil. All law systems have to suppress public evil. We are speaking here of a law to *shape the thinking of another person's children*.

The Gospel Disrupts Families

Jesus warned how powerful His gospel is. It is disruptive of families.

> "Do not think that I came to bring peace on earth. I did not come to bring peace but a sword. For I have come to 'set a man against his father, a daughter against her mother, and a daughter-in-law against her mother-in-law.' And 'a man's foes will be those of his own household' [Micah 7:6]. He who loves father or mother more than Me is not worthy of Me. And he who loves son or daughter more than Me is not worthy of Me" (Matthew 10:34-37).

Thus, any attempt to require by civil law that any non-Christian parent send his children to church is a direct attack on his family. Is such an attack valid, even if the person refuses to instruct his children in the Christian faith? Few Christians today would argue that it is, despite the eternal consequences for the children of rejecting the gospel. The legal integrity of the family must be preserved; the state is to keep out.

Yet there are millions and millions of Christians who vote for politicians who enact laws that compel Christian families to send their children into unsafe, drug-infested, humanist-dominated, anti-Christian sink holes (public schools). These same Christian parents also allow the state to extract tax money to build these schools, pay the salaries of teachers, and forcibly transport their children across town "for reasons of racial balance."

Only this last infringement on family integrity, forcible bussing, has outraged white parents, Christian and non-Christian, which indicates that the commitment to blood lines (race) is the only thing more important to voters than their commitment to public education. This is a sad testimony.

A State-Established Church

What Christians have refused to admit is that the public schools are today a state-established church. The religion they teach is the religion of humanism. It is hidden in the lie that education can be neutral. Christians have bought this lie, and in the name of literacy, they have voted away their families' legal integrity, and the legal integrity of all other families.

What they refuse to do in the name of the gospel of eternal salvation—compel non-Christian parents to send their children to church one hour a week—they gladly do in the name of universal literacy.

But God will not be mocked. The government-financed schools no longer produce universal literacy.

The State Has a Legal Monopoly of Coercion

"Then when they had mocked Him, they took the robe off Him, put His own clothes on Him, and led Him away to be crucified. Now as they came out, they found a man of Cyrene, Simon by name. Him they compelled to bear His cross" (Matthew 27:31-32).

The first step in any long-term program of Christian political action is to decide what the Bible says are the lawful tasks for civil government. We need to know what is prohibited to the state and what is required of the state.

This passage describes an incident in the crucifixion of Christ. We learn what distinguishes civil government from other institutions. Civil governments have the power of force. The soldiers *compelled* Simon of Cyrene to carry our Lord's cross.

The power to use force is clearly given by God to civil rulers. Paul states in Romans 13:1: "the authorities that exist are appointed by God." Paul refers to civil rulers as "ministers of God" and says the ruler "does not bear the sword in vain" (13:4).

Swords were used in ancient times as instruments of death. God has instituted the state and given it the police power. The state not only may use, but *must* use capital punishment to punish evildoers who commit capital crimes, such as premeditated murder and kidnapping.

The power of the sword is strictly limited in the Bible. One of the cliché's popular among conservatives is that we believe in "limited government." The problem is that we seldom say what we mean by the term. Limited to what? Some persons say the government ought to do for the people what the people cannot do for themselves. Who is to say what people cannot do for themselves? By what standard does a society properly make such a determination?

The only proper guide to follow is the Bible. What are the limitations on civil government that are set forth in the Word of God? Paul informs us in Romans 13 that the civil ruler is to be "an avenger to execute wrath on him who practices evil." "For rulers are not a terror to good works, but to evil," Paul states in 13:3. (For more details on Biblical civil government, see Gary DeMar's book in the Biblical Blueprints Series, *Ruler of the Nations*.)

Should the Police Run the Schools?

The answer to this question ought to be obvious. Of course the police should not be running the schools. The police should be out catching criminals and bringing them to justice. The duty of government is to "punish evildoers."

Now suppose we ask the question another way. *Should the county (or city) run a school system?*

"Well, of course it should," many Christians will reply. "After all, how else are the children going to get educated?" We may be given a dozen reasons why the government should be in the education business. The police power of the civil government supposedly must be applied to parents to compel them to educate their children.

Then comes the next argument: "Since some parents just cannot afford to obey this law, the civil government has a moral and legal obligation to supply free schools." How "free" are these schools? As "free of charge" as your property tax bills, paid until you die, whether or not you have school-age children.

The Police Power

It is helpful to know where the word "police" originated. This familiar word comes from the Greek word for "city." In Greek the word is "polis." The Greek word has survived in such names as "Indiana*polis*" and "Deca*polis*." The famous Greek temple, the Parthenon, was built on the Acropolis, which means the highest part of the city.

In ancient Greece, there were city-states such as Athens and Sparta. Today we have cities, towns, counties, states, and other units of civil government. In addition, there is the ever-present Federal government, not to mention efforts to establish one-world government.

The police are hired by governments. Generally we associate the police with local governments. Because the police have so much power (that's why we usually refer to them as the police *force*), we consider it desirable to keep them under the control of our counties and cities. A few years ago the bumper sticker, "Support Your Local Police" was promoted to block the idea of a national police force.

For the same reason that we want local control over the police, we might argue that we should have local control over our schools. Let's have "neighborhood" schools controlled by locally elected officials. I agree that if the schools are going to be run by the government, then local control is best. But why should government at any level operate the schools? Civil governments are given the power of force, the police power, to punish evildoers.

The public school system is based on the idea of force. It should be called a *government* school system because it is run by the government. In effect, the civil government or public schools are operated by the police. It does not matter that the persons in charge in the classrooms are called teachers or that there are principals and superintendents over them. They are able to operate as they do only because they have the police power, the power of force.

Coercive Education

The public school system operates on the principle of compulsion in two respects: compulsory attendance laws to force the students to come, and compulsory taxation to force the taxpayers to pay the bill. The two go together. Because school attendance is mandatory, the money to operate the school is mandatory. In a later chapter, I will discuss the financing of the public school system. For now, let us focus our attention on the compulsory attendance laws.

Compulsory attendance laws have been on the books since the beginning in the state of Massachusetts. The Puritans passed a compulsory attendance law in 1647:

> "It is therefore ordered, that every township in this jurisdiction, after the Lord hath increased them to the number of fifty households, shall then forthwith appoint one within their town to teach all such children as shall resort to him to read and write, whose wages shall be paid either by the parents or masters of such children, or by the inhabitants in general. . . ."

It was this long tradition of compulsory Christian education, which was in part financed by the taxing authority of the civil government, that two centuries later served Horace Mann so well in his call to establish taxpayer-financed non-Christian schools in Massachusetts.

Taxpayer-financed education in the southern United States came in full force after the South lost the Civil War in 1865. Compulsory education laws were dropped briefly in the late 1950's and early 1960's, when massive resistance to racial integration was in style. The state of Virginia did not have compulsory attendance in these years, and possibly some other states dropped compulsory attendance laws for a period of time. To my knowledge, all states now have such laws. The wording of the laws varies from state to state.

Enforcing What Most People Already Do

It should be understood that it is difficult in a nation that has a democratic or republican form of government to get voters to support civil measures that they do not support privately. An illiterate nation is unlikely to vote for compulsory school laws. Only where there is already a high degree of literacy in a society will voters approve universal, taxpayer-financed education.

What the vast majority of people have already done for their own children — taught them to read — they then vote to make compulsory on the tiny minority of citizens or residents who have refused to imitate the majority voluntarily. Thus, compulsory attendance laws can do very little to improve a nation's educational standards. As we have seen for two generations in the United States, the nation's literacy rate has actually dropped.

Legalized Kidnapping and Desertion

The discussion of school attendance laws never centers around whether there ought to be such laws, but rather what should be the age limits and what exceptions, if any, ought to be allowed. The government, in effect, claims the children at all ages. Just as government claims all our income and exempts some from taxation, so political leaders claim our children from birth. The debate in the legislatures is only over the age at which children must attend school, the hours of attendance, and the number of days per year. The legislature of Virginia has even decreed that school must not begin until after Labor Day. The purpose of this law is to "Keep Virginia Green" by luring the local tourists to spend for one more holiday weekend. Literacy is one thing, but tourism is *really* important politically.

The trend in recent years has been to require children to attend school at an ever-younger age. There are several reasons for this. The humanists want to get the children away from their parents sooner. They consider some of the kids "hopeless reactionaries" by the time they are six years old. The children have been "indoctrinated" so much by their parents that the school has difficulty re-educating them.

Another reason for earlier school entrance is that more parents are going to work, so they want taxpayer-financed babysitting as soon as possible.

Perhaps the most important reason is that if early taxpayer-financed education isn't available, the parents will start their children in private schools. They may decide to keep them in the private schools after they reach the compulsory school age.

When I started my Christian school in 1961, there was no kindergarten program in the Fairfax County school system. I started one. We had the children reading by the time they were ready to enter the first grade. Parents hesitated to enroll their children in the local government school to be taught the material the children had already learned. So they kept them in my school. This story was repeated in numerous Christian schools.

So Fairfax County started a kindergarten program. The children were not taught to read, but they were kept out of Christian schools that would have taught them to read.

Coercive Root, Third-Rate Fruit

Here is a partial list of problems caused by compulsory attendance laws:

1. Parents who want to educate their children at home find themselves being treated as criminals.

2. Private schools are harassed in various ways. Since children must attend school, the state finds it necessary to define what a "school" is. The logical outcome is an endless stream of regulations dealing with teacher qualifications, curriculum, days and hours of operation, etc., etc. The schools that don't knuckle under are then targeted for further police action.

3. Children are sent to school whether they want to be there or not. A case might be made that a six year old should not be choosing whether to go to school or out to play, but a 17 year old is a different matter. The schools are stuck with bored teenagers who haven't the slightest interest in the education being offered. They become rebellious, disrupt the classes, lower the morale of the teachers, and in numerous ways make a general nuisance of themselves. (The police are not far away though. I mean the uniformed kind. They are sent into the classrooms to control the crime. The real crime is forcing these kids into the classroom in the first place. An even worse crime is requiring decent kids to have to associate with these hoods. And another crime on top of this is making everybody else pay the bill.)

4. Parents, children, and the public are lulled into believing

that the students have received an education. After all, they have
attended school for the prescribed number of years and have now
received a diploma. Many of them can not read their diploma,
but who cares? The state says they are educated. They have graduated from accredited schools with certified teachers.

5. Because school attendance is compulsory, the state must
provide it. And it is all free! *Free public education!* How many times
have we heard this? Yet there is nothing free about it. Public education is very expensive. It wastes the lives of students — the major
cost of public education. It reduces the God-given authority of the
parents, thereby reducing their sense of personal responsibility for
their children — another hidden cost. Finally, the money to pay for
it does not come from charity either. Compulsory school attendance leads directly to compulsory financing (spelled "t-a-x-e-s").

Compulsory Education is a Failure

"Prove it," you say. I could cite all kinds of statistics, data,
reports, studies, books, and articles from within the educational
establishment to prove the existence of massive failure. But every
literate person who has read anything in the newspapers about
public education already knows about these reports. The public
schools are getting a D on their report cards, even though the people grading them are generally favorable towards taxpayer-
financed education. President Reagan's special commission on
education found the public school so terribly deficient that its
report was dismally entitled "A Nation at Risk."

I could also find plenty of proof from other sources as well. I
don't intend to do that. Others have made the point. Rudolph
Flesch wrote his famous *Why Johnny Can't Read* in the 1950's. Years
later he wrote *Why Johnny Still Can't Read*. Johnny can't spell either.
And he can't add and subtract or do a whole lot of things. So why
beat a dead horse? We all know about the failure of the public
schools.

The debate begins when we try to assess proper *responsibility*
for the failure. The defenders refuse to admit that it is the compulsory nature of modern education that has led to the failure.

For well over a century, the failure of the schools has been explained away by employees of the schools in terms of one answer: "More Money Needed Here." This is another way for them to point at your wallet and mine, and announce: "Less Money Needed There."

If a particular year or model of a car gains a reputation of being a "lemon," would it be smart for the company to raise its price before it finds out what is wrong with the car? If, after a hundred years of trying to get some product improved, its performance gets worse, should its producer raise its price by 15% each year?

There is only one way that the producer could get away with such a pricing policy: *compel people to buy it.* That is the long and the short of the massive, visible failure of public education.

But how do we know for certain that compulsory education is a failure? After all, the public schools are spending a lot of money on education. They have impressive buildings. More and more students are going on to college. I have just one question to ask. *If public schools are so successful, why do we have to force children to attend?*

The promise of public education is similar to the promise of Communism. The Soviet Union is always telling us how wonderful communism is. If this really is the case, then why don't they tear down the Iron Curtain and put in a picture window? Why do they have to erect a wall around East Berlin to keep the residents from running away? Why would anyone want to escape from a worker's paradise? Why do they vote with their feet? The answer is obvious.

As applied to education, I ask the question again. If the education offered by government schools is all that good, then why do they send the police to round up the kids who aren't in attendance? After all, tuition for public education is zero. Parents pay taxes whether their children attend public schools or not. If taxpayer-financed education is both good and free, then why does anyone need to be forced to get it for his children? Are people so stupid that they don't know what a nice deal is when they see it?

Another question comes to mind. Why are all these families voting against the public schools with their pocketbooks? Why are they paying taxes to the public schools for "the best education money can buy," and then shelling out tuition money on top of that in order to send their children to a private school? Are they so rich that they don't miss the money? Are they snobs who send their kids to private schools for status?

Let me answer some of these questions. The parents who are choosing the private schools for their children are not rich. For the most part, they are just average on the economic ladder. Vance Packard in *The Status Seekers* admits that the rich are sending their kids to the public schools. The idea that private schools are just for the rich may have been true several decades ago. It isn't today. Parents are selecting the non-public schools because *they are convinced their children are getting a better education in those schools*. These parents are making decisions based on personal experience with both kinds of schools. They are more aware of the teaching that takes place in the government schools. As a result, they are making the sacrifices necessary to obtain a better education for their children.

On Playing Hookey

When I was in elementary school, I learned about playing hookey. That was a rarity in our four-room country school because we had a mean principal. If you got a licking in school, you could also figure on getting another one when you got home. The parents backed the principal.

Times have changed. We still have compulsory school laws, but hookey playing has greatly increased. In many of our large city school systems, as many as one-fourth of the students will be truant on any given day. The public schools of the District of Columbia decided to have school on Good Friday in 1986. (Probably they think having a holiday then is mixing education with Christianity.) Fifty per cent of the students didn't come to class. Forty per cent of the teachers failed to attend!

They say you can lead a horse to water, but you can't make

him drink. In the case of the students, it is difficult even to get him to the water of learning. When you get him there, you can't make him think. It is easy to pass laws. (Well, not all that easy. I served in the Virginia legislature, and they sure didn't want to pass the bills I introduced.) It is something else again to enforce them. The country is full of missing children (most of them carried off by a parent). The authorities can't locate them, let alone keep tabs on every kid on the block.

Even if they can get the kids in school, the teachers may find that students aren't functioning because they are hungry, or on dope, or mentally out of it for some other reason. The compulsory attendance laws are a failure. Their only success, from a humanistic point of view, has been their use in making life difficult for Christian parents who want to take charge of the education of their offspring.

The Biblical Alternative to Compulsory School Laws

The Biblical alternative to compulsory school laws is to abolish them! Who needs them?

"Ah," you say, "but what about all the children who won't get an education if you do away with the compulsory school laws?" My answer is this. There are millions of children who are not getting an education now under the compulsory school laws. The percentage of functional illiterates today is probably higher than it was in the era of the American Revolution, when there were few public schools outside of New England. God will not be mocked.

The Christian alternative is for parents to assume their responsibility for the education of their children. We are not to think that we are wiser than God. God has given parents the task of bringing up their children in the nurture and admonition of the Lord. They may and should use the compulsion of the rod if necessary to train up the children. This is the rod of reproof. It is the discipline of the parents. It is not to be confused with the power of the sword given by God to civil rulers.

Because the financing is different, public vs. private, the structure of authority is different. Therefore, the whole educational atmosphere is different. The school now operates in a climate of voluntary exchange between those operating the school and the parents who are engaging the services of the school to aid in carrying out their God-given responsibilities.

Christians Are Responsible

We are in a war for the hearts and souls of men. It has been going on since Eden.

Christ, by His death and resurrection, regained the deed to the world that Adam had forfeited to Satan. Christians are therefore to exercise greater and greater dominion. In a "fair fight," meaning an unsubsidized, noncoercive competitive struggle, Christianity will defeat all rivals. Unfortunately, few Christians seem to believe this. Jesus said that He had been given all authority in heaven and earth (Matthew 28:18). Christians for a long time haven't seemed to understand that, either. This is at last beginning to change.

If your children were competing against Communists for a job, would you vote to have your taxes raised, in order to give the money to the sons and daughters of Communists? If the Communists were illiterate, and you were willing to finance your children's education, would you regard this as a bad thing?

Why not allow people to follow their views concerning God, man, law, and the future? Why not allow people to finance their own visions of the future? Why not allow responsible Christians to triumph over their irresponsible enemies?

The only answer that Christian intellectuals give is some version of: "Through the coercive power of civil government, Christians morally and legally owe a tax-subsidized education to God's enemies." We don't. We owe them equal justice before God's revealed law, nothing else. Civil law should not compel any parent to send his children to school, any more than it should compel them to send their children to church or Communist indoctrination schools.

Abolish the public schools, and Christians will take over the country and the world that much faster. This is what worries

Satan. Why should it worry Christians?

Does it worry you? Why?

Summary

Christians have been lured by good intentions to vote for a system of compulsory education that the humanists have captured. The humanists have used the tyranny implicit in compulsory education to indoctrinate the children of the Christians.

Compulsory attendance laws are no different in principle from compulsory church attendance laws, once we acknowledge that all education is religious, and that no education is religiously neutral. This is acknowledged by more and more Christians, as well as more and more humanists. Yet Christians continue to support the idea of compulsory education. This is irrational. It is also very expensive for taxpayers.

In summary:

1. Biblical law requires people to understand and obey civil law.

2. Biblical law does not require every person to attend a Trinitarian church.

3. For centuries, western societies did not understand this principle of freedom of conscience.

4. Civil government is not to enforce positive good; it is supposed to restrain public evil.

5. It is not the responsibility of one group of citizens to enforce particular religious ideas on the children of other voters.

6. There can never be neutral education; all education is inherently religious.

7. It is therefore not the responsibility of one group of parents to enforce a particular education on the children of other parents.

8. The question of making irresponsible parents do this or that about their children's instruction is irrelevant from the point of view of Biblical civil law.

9. The integrity of the family must be preserved.

10. No man may lawfully force another person's child to accept a particular view of God, man, or time.

11. Biblical civil law only restricts public evil acts.

12. Christians nevertheless support the idea of neutral public education.

13. The civil government is God's lawful monopoly of coercion.

14. Should the policeman run the schools?

15. Compulsory school attendance laws are an infringement on parental authority.

16. They are the equivalent of compulsory church attendance laws.

17. Christians nevertheless support compulsory attendance laws.

18. Compulsory attendance is a form of legalized kidnapping.

19. Coercive education is third-rate education.

20. If state education is so good, why do we need laws to require attendance?

21. Christian dominion is the goal for Christians.

22. If irresponsible humanists refuse to educate their children, what is that to us?

23. Why should we subsidize the education of our mortal enemies' children?

24. They want us to subsidize their teaching our children the principles of humanism.

25. Christians nevertheless support compulsory attendance laws.

26. Why?

6

SALVATION IS BY GRACE, NOT BY EDUCATION

So the Egyptians pursued them [the Israelites], all the horses
and chariots of Pharaoh, his horsemen and his army, and overtook
them camping by the sea (Exodus 14:9).

Even though one disaster after another struck Pharaoh, his
heart was not changed. He reluctantly agreed to let God's people
have their freedom after the final plague (the slaying of the first-
born) came upon the Egyptians. The Israelites had barely left the
land when Pharaoh sent his army to pursue them. His goal was to
put them back into bondage, to exercise complete control over
them.

The Pharaoh was looked upon as god on earth by the Egyptians. Egyptian society was based on the idea of slavery. This is
why the Pharaohs built the pyramids. The pyramid was a symbol
of the Egyptian power religion. The top of the pyramid repre-
sented the Pharaoh. He was the link between heaven and earth.
He was the absolute ruler over all. Beneath him were the people.
He ruled by raw power.

Because Pharaoh believed he was absolute, he wanted to en-
slave all around him. When men deny that the state is under God,
they invariably teach that the state is divine. The German philosopher Hegel said, "The state is god walking on earth." Modern
power states consider themselves to be god.

As god, power states claim sovereignty. They consider themselves lord of all. They want to be omniscient (to know all things).
This is why they conduct a census to collect all kinds of informa-

tion. They want to foreordain the future. This is why they establish planning commissions. They want to be omnipotent (all-powerful). This is why they try to control everything.

The Religion of the Public Schools

"Then Paul stood in the midst of the Areopagus and said, 'Men of Athens, I perceive that in all things you are very religious'" (Acts 17:22).

John Dewey is considered to have had more influence on modern public school education than any other person. Dewey was a professing atheist and a socialist. Yet he stated that it is up to America's public schools to save our threatened religious heritage.

That sounds strange, coming from the pen of a person who was an unbeliever. We have heard it said so often, "Religion has been taken out of the public schools."

Was Dewey wrong? Did he want religion in the schools? If so, why have his followers thrown out any traces of the *Christian* religion? No, Dewey's program was right on target. Dewey wanted the *religion of humanism* in the state schools, and that is exactly what we have in the United States today. The public schools are anti-Christian. They are not anti-religious.

The original model for public schools around the world is still operating, the *Ecole Polytechnique* of Paris. It was created by the successors of the French Revolution. In 1795, the last year of the guillotining of thousands of Frenchmen, the government of France centralized all secondary education, meaning all higher education. They created a series of schools ("ecoles") that were firmly under government control.

The *Ecole Polytechnique* had been set up in 1794. Under the new administration, it became the science and technology institute for France. The ruling vision was that of engineering. Men were taught to view all of society as a vast machine. They were taught that "social engineering" is possible, and that a top-down planning system could bring productivity and power to France. This is the ancient power religion of Egypt and Satan, but it was dressed up in scientific clothing. It was dressed up in the language of scientific neutrality.

This school taught religion, the religion of scientific humanism. It believed in blueprints—not *moral* blueprints, but rather scientific planning blueprints. Professor F. A. Hayek has written about the *Ecole Polytechnique* in his book, *The Counter-Revolution of Science*. He writes: "The whole teaching centered, to a much higher degree than is still true of similar institutions, around . . . descriptive geometry, or the art of blue-print making. . . ."

Everyone Has a Religion

When Paul came to Athens, he was encountered by philosophers from the Epicureans and the Stoics. In their view, Paul believed in "strange gods." Paul noted the "devotions" of these pagan Greek philosophers. He also commented on their altar with the inscription "TO THE UNKNOWN GOD." He referred to them as being "very religious" (Acts 17:22).

What would Paul say about the public school philosophers of our day? I think he would consider them very religious, too. The problem with the world today is not a lack of religion. The problem is the wrong kind of religion.

People are naturally religious. They worship someone or something. They have a faith. Public schools are not devoid of religion. They are very religious. They are based on a false religion. That religion is secular humanism. It is the worship of man.

A study of John Dewey will reveal that democracy was his religion. Democracy is "rule by the people." This is a form of humanism. Dewey wanted the public schools to believe in that which is common to men and society. Anything that brings differences is to be eliminated. Christianity had to go because it brings division. Secular humanism results in a least-common-denominator religion. It leads to a leveling of man. The leveling is accomplished by constantly lowering standards, whether they are religious, moral, or academic. Christian philosopher Cornelius Van Til has called this "integration downward into the void."

There is plenty of evidence to show that public schools are religious. R. J. Rushdoony in his scholarly study, *The Messianic Character of American Education* (1963), traces educational philosophy from Horace Mann down to the present. As Rushdoony notes, the various gurus of American public education constantly use religious terminology in describing their goals. They speak of saving man. State teacher training schools are even called "the coming of the Lord."

Evolution has replaced creation as the explanation for the origin of life on earth. The state, as the most powerful human institution, becomes the evolving god of the public schools. Schools are financed by the humanistic, "neutral" state; they therefore serve the needs of the state. Children are taught to serve the state. The state is to plan and control the future. The state becomes the final authority and source of law. As Rushdoony says, whatever the source of law is in a society, that is its god.

Secular humanism has become the new established religion in the United States, and the public schools have become the established church. Tax money is used to support this established church. The teachers have become the priests and priestesses of this new church. Even the black robes associated with the priests and judges have been appropriated by the schools to symbolize their claims, even though they are worn only on graduation day or at special occasions.

The Myth of Neutrality

A common belief is that public schools are neutral when it comes to religion. This is the reason given by many Christians for sending their children to such schools.

Neutrality is a myth. Jesus said that we are either for Him or against Him. We cannot serve God and mammon. There is no middle ground or neutral zone.

No area of life is outside God's interest or control. To believe in neutrality is to believe that God is confined to only part of the universe. His specially revealed law rules in this limited area, but everywhere else a common law is in control, a law that everyone in principle can understand (or at least highly educated people — "priests" — can understand and then tell the rest of us). In other words, the world is sort of like a giant machine, with its laws enforced impersonally by "Nature." (Shades of the *Ecole Polytechnique*!)

The Christian cannot accept this viewpoint. The notion that science, mathematics, reading, or any other area can be separated from God is fallacious. When humanism is consistently applied in the schools, it will necessarily have certain ill effects. When Christianity is consistently applied, it will necessarily have beneficial effects.

The humanist view looks upon man as the object of worship. This is why it is called "*human*ism." Whatever the humanist calls his god is of no importance. *Humanism is the worship of man.* The humanist god will only be a projection of man in one form or another. There is no place in the humanist religion for the true and living God who *reveals* Himself to man both in the natural world and also in the written word, the Bible.

The humanist regards the Bible as just another book. This is why the humanistic schools would study the Bible as literature, but nothing more. Children might be allowed to study about Christianity, but never must they pray to God or worship Him in any way at school. This is directly contrary to humanist doctrine.

The humanists believe the earth originated by chance. God has no place in the world and does not control the world. Man is in control. The humanist believes man originated by chance in a process of blind evolution. Man has animal origins, according to this thinking.

There is no place for sin in the humanist scheme of things. There are no moral absolutes. Morals are relative. Right or wrong may be decided by majority vote, government edict, or what an individual may feel is "right for him" at the time.

When the Commonwealth (State) of Kentucky passed legislation allowing the Ten Commandments to be posted in public school classrooms, the humanists were quick to take the case to the Supreme Court of the United States. The humanists won. There is no place for Biblical morality in the humanist system. Any similarity between Biblical morality and humanist morality is purely coincidental.

Religion affects morality. The basis of Christian morality is

the Bible. The Bible was given by God. God tells us in His Word
what sin is. He tells us what is right and what is wrong. The
Christian religion determines the moral standards a Christian is
to follow.

The humanistic religion has a different standard of morality.
For example, the humanist believes man is an animal. The
humanist denies the historicity of Adam and Eve. There was no
historical Fall into sin. Man is not born with a sinful nature. As a
result of this humanist belief, the humanist considers man's problems to be his environment. Man becomes only an animal to be
conditioned and controlled by his environment. So the humanist
works to change man's environment by legislation. The humanist
tries to create a paradise on earth by using the state to change
man. He believes in *social engineering*. This is why control of the
schools is so dear to the heart of the humanist.

Public schools today speak of the teachers as "change agents."
The schools talk a lot about "values clarification." These are just
fancy words to disguise the plans of the government schools to
root out what Christian ideas are left in the students.

Humanist education legally rests on the idea of neutrality.
They need this myth to justify compulsory education. Yet they
teach moral relativism, an affront to Christian parents. Thus,
they need the myth of neutrality, yet they openly teach the religion of moral relativism. The schools are schizophrenic.

Humanism's War on Christian Schools

Over a century ago, a dedicated humanist scholar named
Lester Frank Ward outlined the foundation of modern public
school education. He was an evolutionist, a sociologist, and chief
paleontologist (a student of fossils) for the U.S. Geological Sur-
vey. He earned academic degrees in medicine, law, and the arts.
He was a statistician, and worked in the U.S. Treasury Department. He later was elected the first president of the American
Sociological Association. He was a great believer in state education. He spelled out in clear detail what he expected public school
teachers to do: whatever the state commands. Here is what he

wrote in volume 2 of his book, *Dynamic Sociology* (1883).

> The secret of the superiority of state over private education lies in the fact that in the former the teacher is responsible solely to society. As in private, so also in public education, the calling of the teacher is a profession, and his personal success must depend upon his success in accomplishing the result which his employers desire accomplished. But the result desired by the state is a wholly different one from that desired by parents, guardians, and pupils. Of the latter he is happily independent. This independence renders him practically free. His own ideas of method naturally harmonize more or less completely with those of the state (pp. 589-90).

> Lastly, public education is immeasurably better for society. It is so because it really accomplishes the object of education, which private education does not. What society most needs is the distribution of the knowledge in its possession. This is a work which can not be trusted to individuals. It can neither be left to the discretion of children, of parents, nor of teachers. It is not for any of these to say what knowledge is most useful to society. No tribunal short of that which society in its sovereign capacity shall appoint is competent to decide this question. To the teacher duly trained for his work may be left certain questions of method, especially of detail; but even the method must be in its main features unified with a view to the greatest economy of application. This must necessarily also be the duty of the supreme authority (p. 591).

And just what is this "supreme authority"? *The state.* Society exists only where there is civil government and legislation. "Only where actual legislation is conducted can there be said to exist a complete social organism. Wherever any such complete social organism exists, it is possible to conceive of true scientific legislation" (p. 397).

It is not surprising to learn that Ward hated Christianity. He actually said that all religious leaders who have claimed divine inspiration "must be referred not only to a pathological but to an actually deranged condition of their minds" (Vol. 1, p. 12). And he promised: "The school will fill the place now occupied by the church" (Vol. 1, p. 27).

This is a rival religion. What kinds of fruit has it produced? By their fruits, ye shall know them, Jesus said.

Moral Problems in the Public Schools

The public schools are full of moral problems. There are reasons for this. The primary reason (hidden to the public) is that secular humanism is a religion of destruction: the destruction of Christianity, and therefore the destruction of everything that Christianity has made possible, meaning Western civilization. But this destructive side of secular humanism is never discussed in public by humanist educators. Most of the people the public sees probably do not even recognize this side of humanism. Marxists do, and radical atheists do, but not your average teacher.

The secondary reason why the schools have moral problems is that the modern philosophy of education denies that there are any permanent moral standards. They teach this philosophy very well. The students learn it, and then as they mature, they begin to act in terms of it.

Suicide

The most common cause of death (other than accidents) among students in the United States is suicide. The students find no reason to live. Humanism destroys meaning and purpose. If there is no God who judges men finally in terms of His eternal standards of right and wrong, then where is man to discover purpose? If mankind is going to die when the sun dies, or the universe dies, then what is the meaning of life? Meaning has to be found in something that is greater than life on earth if it is to have any authority over the affairs of life. But humanism denies any final or present authority to any process or Being that is beyond evolutionary processes in this world.

Why would schools today need extensive counselling about death? I think the answer lies in the humanist religion of the public schools. The children have not been taught to face the real world, for the real world is a world of death. It brings the death of men, and it will eventually bring the death of Man, evolutionists teach. The humanist has his faith in Man with a capital "M." He puts his trust in chariots, in princes, in earthly things. He therefore puts his trust in death: Man who dies.

Drugs

The drug problem is a common one in the public schools. The answer to the problem has generally been to provide "drug education" courses. The problem only gets worse. The students probably already know more about drugs than their teachers. The problem is not a lack of knowledge. The problem is a lack of godly faith. The public schools are trying to save the children through knowledge. The Bible says that "The *fear of the* LORD is the beginning of knowledge" (Proverbs 1:7).

This is why drug education is not the answer to the drug problem. The same can be said about cigarette smoking. The wrapper says plainly, "The Surgeon General has determined that cigarette smoking is harmful to your health." But people keep right on smoking.

Teenage Pregnancy

Teenage pregnancy is a major problem in the government schools. The humanist answer? Sex education classes become part of the curriculum. Birth control devices are made available to the students. Abortion is promoted. Is the problem solved? No! The reason is that the secular public schools are not working on the solution.

The solution is Biblical: the message of Christ's faithfulness to His church, and a man's faithfulness to his wife. The solution is *sex within marriage*, taught as an explicitly Biblical religious principle. This Biblical principle is to be taught and enforced by the church (excommunication), taught and enforced by the state (laws against polygamy and adultery), and taught and enforced by the family. But the public schools are not teaching this Biblical principle. They are "religiously neutral" by law. They teach anti-Biblical principles of human sexuality. They are a big part of the problem themselves. Humanism won't solve the problem because humanism is not true.

Pragmatism

One of the popular philosophies of our day is "pragmatism." Pragmatism is the idea that if something "works" it is true. But what do they mean, "works." *By what standard* do they determine if something really works? You see, they are not neutral. They have a doctrine of good and bad, acceptable and unacceptable, hidden behind their "neutral" pragmatism.

Jesus said, "By their fruits ye shall know them." Christianity is true and it produces good fruits. We don't believe it because it produces good fruits. We believe it because God has revealed truth to us. If pragmatists were consistent, they would embrace Christianity because Christianity works. They don't embrace Christianity. The pragmatists in the public schools are so blinded by their official philosophy of neutrality that they cannot officially judge whether something works. But they do in reality. We all do. But they do so on the basis of a taxpayer-financed lie: the theory of neutrality.

Work Ethic

The moral climate of the government schools carries over into academics. In the very beginning, God instituted work (Genesis 2). It is central to man's life on earth. God placed Adam in the Garden of Eden. He told him to dress the garden and keep it. Adam was to have dominion over the earth. When Adam sinned, the Lord cursed Adam's work because that was at the center of his existence.

What has been called the "Protestant work ethic" is basic to all human progress. School is an important preparation for man's task of subduing the earth. It involves work at school and work (called homework) at home.

Humanistic education has downplayed the idea of work. Even some book titles reflect the idea that school should be easy. Remember *Fun With Dick and Jane*? This bias against work is seen in the report cards and promotion practices of the schools. Letter and number grades have given place to vague terms such as "Satisfactory" and "Unsatisfactory." I was always intrigued with

"Needs Improvement." After all, who doesn't? We have had serious grade inflation in the government schools.

The result has been graduates who expect everything in life to be easy. They don't want to do yard work because that is "too sweaty." Many of our young people are unemployed, even when there are "Help Wanted" signs all over the place.

A Loss of Vision

The whole idea of progress comes from a religious belief that God is in control and that He wants man to subdue the earth and have dominion over it. Without meaning and purpose in the universe, man is reduced to the level of an animal struggling merely to survive. Even bare survival is questioned by some. There is no way the government schools can produce over any period of time with their humanistic foundation. It is a foundation of sand and can not sustain a civilization.

What is the real purpose of the public schools? Are they merely babysitting institutions? The best they can come up with is that they want to train young people to be "good citizens." What is meant by "good"? Is it merely to get along with one's fellow man? If that is the case, then they are not doing very well. A public school philosopher said that we are uncertain where we are going, and why we are doing what we are doing. That fairly well sums it up.

The reason the secularized government schools can function at all is that they are not always consistent with their own premises. They are still influenced by the culture around them. God restrains the evil of man. He never allows us to live as wickedly as we wish.

There is a better way. That is through the Christian school.

Summary

The power religion has been at war with God's dominion religion from the beginning. We see it best illustrated in Bible history in the Book of Exodus. The Pharaoh was the manifestation of power religion.

When the state becomes the educator, it must adopt one aspect of the power religion. People are compelled to send their children into non-neutral schools. In our day, this has meant that Christian parents have been forced to finance the indoctrination of most children (including their own) with a rival religion, the humanist religion of evolutionism.

A war is going on that Christians have begun to recognize only in the last two decades. This has threatened the public schools as nothing has threatened them in American history. Yet the majority of Christian voters still do not recognize the nature of the religious battle, nor the moral issue of compulsory attendance.

In summary:

1. Egyptian religion was power religion.
2. They believed the state is the agency of salvation.
3. Paul called the Greeks of Athens religious.
4. Modern education is "Greek": supposedly based on neutral reason.
5. John Dewey wanted humanist religion in the public schools, and only humanist religion.
6. Modern education is based on the "lowest common denominator" principle.
7. Evolution has replaced creation as the explanation of origins.
8. Evolution also has replaced the doctrine of God's providence with the gospel of science-controlled evolution.
9. Students are taught to respect the state, the new sovereign over our world.
10. The myth of neutrality is the legal basis of public education.
11. Neutrality is a myth.
12. Therefore, the public schools are caught in a dilemma: they need neutrality, yet they cannot get it if everything is relative (as they teach).
13. The public schools are at war with Christianity.
14. The public schools have serious moral problems as a direct result of their humanist beliefs.
15. The humanists are losing faith in the future.
16. The Christian school movement can now offer a better education.

7

CHRISTIAN SCHOOLS MUST
RESIST STATE CERTIFICATION

And Jeroboam said in his heart, "Now the kingdom may return to the house of David: If these people go up to offer sacrifices in the house of the LORD at Jerusalem, then the heart of this people will turn back to their lord, Rehoboam king of Judah, and they will kill me and go back to Rehoboam king of Judah." Therefore the king took counsel and made two calves of gold, and said to the people, "It is too much for you to go up to Jerusalem. Here are your gods, O Israel, which brought you up from the land of Egypt!" And he set up one in Bethel, and the other he put in Dan. Now this thing became a sin, for the people went to worship before the one as far as Dan. He made shrines on the high places, and made priests from every class of people, who were not of the sons of Levi (1 Kings 12:26-31).

Jeroboam had just created a successful political and military revolt against Rehoboam, son of Solomon, who had foolishly and rebelliously threatened to impose heavy additional taxes on the nation of Israel. Jeroboam led ten of the twelve tribes into revolt.

Jeroboam was no fool. He understood that a successful military revolt cannot be sustained long enough to become a true revolution unless the hearts of the people are changed religiously and morally. Military power is not enough. The people will drift back to the politics of the past if their spiritual hearts are still looking to the past. This was the same problem Moses faced with the Israelites in the wilderness. It was solved only when the original generation of slaves died (except Joshua and Caleb), and the future-looking second generation marched into Canaan.

Jeroboam saw a way to gain the hearts of his people. He recognized that they had very poor theology. They were therefore already in partial ethical rebellion against God. So he played to the crowd's worst impulses. He adopted a "lowest common denominator" theology. He returned ritually to the wicked theology of Egypt, and had golden calves built. These, he said, had delivered them from Egypt.

The public bought it. They wanted to believe it, and he made it easy for them. He built a new system of corrupt worship in order to solidify his own political power. Like the dog that returns to its vomit (2 Peter 2:22), so did the people of Israel return to the corrupt theology of the wilderness rebellion.

The original philosophers of the humanist public school movement hated Christianity. They knew it was their supreme enemy, but they also knew that most Americans were Christians. Their incredibly successful strategy was to adopt the model of Prussia's anti-Christian (Hegelian) state school system. Officially neutral religiously, taxpayer-financed schools would adopt the religion of humanism as a substitute for Christianity. They would teach "good citizenship." They would teach universal morality. They would not discriminate against anyone's religion.

Just like Jeroboam's golden calves wouldn't discriminate against God, and just so long as nobody tried to call the people back to the Bible-believing faith of their fathers.

Also like Jeroboam's political theology, the goal of humanism is to get people to obey the state. Jeroboam wanted the people to obey a new state. The humanists in the 19th century wanted Christians to obey the humanist state, and they took over a dangerous Puritan institution, the compulsory, taxpayer-financed local school, as their chosen instrument of oppression. The golden calf had already been built. They just took over title.

In the light of this humanist strategy, we need to consider some of the ways that secular governments try to control Christian schools.

Licensure

Governments license about everything and everybody these days. They license cars, boats, trucks, dogs, doctors, nurses, businesses, barbers, and builders. About the only groups not licensed are cats and clergymen, both of which put up too much fuss to make it worthwhile.

Would you go to an unlicensed physician for heart surgery? After reading a recent *Wall Street Journal* article, I'm not sure I would go to one who was licensed. It seems there are some quacks in the profession who have managed one way or the other to get a license. What I would like to have is a statement from a legally liable private insurance company that a particular physician is insured by them. They have a direct incentive to make sure the people they insure are competent.

There are quacks in every profession and they can cause you a lot of harm. I read about a man who was run over by an unlicensed driver in an unregistered car. I have read far more accounts of persons being run over by licensed drivers in registered cars. Even licensed persons have been known to get run over by registered cars driven by licensed drivers. To make matters worse, government officials have been known to have accidents in government owned vehicles. No, I'm not trying to make fun of anybody. I just think we need to think a bit about what is involved in licensure.

A local private school always displayed prominently in its advertising that it was "State Licensed." My wife and I used to chuckle about that because we were rather proud of the fact that we were not "State Licensed." For some strange reason, our enrollment kept doubling every year (though you understand that couldn't keep up forever, or else everybody on earth would be enrolled in our school in a few years), while that "State Licensed" school hardly grew at all.

What is licensure anyway? Licensure involves permission. By granting you a license, the state is *permitting* you to do something. If you want to drive a car on the state's highway, you had better get a license. If you want to get married, you will need a license.

(Have you ever wondered why you need a state license to get married? Does the state own the family? That is the key question Ray Sutton's book addresses in the Biblical Blueprint Series: *Who Owns the Family?* I find it interesting that as a minister I must be bonded to perform weddings. You have to get a birth certificate and your heirs have to get you a death certificate. They've got you coming and going.)

The Sileven Case

When a school is licensed, the state is saying it has permission to exist. Pastor Everett Sileven of Faith Baptist Church in Louisville, Nebraska, was tossed into jail in 1983 because he was running a church school without a license from the state.

Why didn't Sileven get a license? He refused licensure because an important principle was at stake. To take a license from the state meant that Pastor Sileven agreed that the state had the right to permit the school to exist. In Sileven's case, it was more than the school. The school was a ministry of the church. The State of Nebraska was saying that it had the right to license a ministry of the church.

It was only the outrage of Christians all over the United States that pressured the state to repeal all laws infringing upon parental choice in schools. The videotape footage of the sheriff taking Sileven to jail mobilized the Christians when it was shown on Christian television shows and in churches. Even the humanist media visited Nebraska and called the government's actions into question. The politicians were being embarrassed publicly month after month. They hated the public exposure. Finally, the Federal court of appeals declared that the state had violated Sileven's civil rights and the rights of dozens of ministers who had been forcibly dragged out of the church. Then the sheriff had a heart attack and retired.

If Christians in Nebraska had rolled over and played dead, the state bureaucrats would have treated them as political corpses. When we Christians act as though we were doormats, the humanists wipe their feet on us. But the Bible says that God treats His enemies as footstools (Psalm 110:1).

The secular humanists are always bleating about the need to separate church and state. They are wolves in sheep's clothing. They did not initially lift a hand to defend Sileven's tiny congregation. Only when the videotapes ("Eyewitness News!") started appearing on national television and in churches did the politicians and educational bureaucrats think twice. The state branch of the National Education Association trade union, the nation's largest political lobby, never did acknowledge that Sileven's case involved basic religious rights. They fought the backtracking politicians all the way.

The Constitution of the United States says that Congress shall make no law respecting an establishment of religion. Nor can Congress or the states prohibit the free exercise of religion. The issue goes beyond the Constitution, however. Under Biblical law, the church is an institution under the authority of God. The king could not usurp priestly functions.

Pastor Sileven won his case. The state has backed off. That doesn't mean the licensing battle is over. It will come up again and again.

What Licensing Implies

Some Christians don't understand the implications of licensing a church. They think that it does not differ from getting a license for your car or your dog. The whole matter of licensing all kinds of professions is outside the scope of this book. Hopefully, God's people will at least realize that the church must never look to the state for its legal right to exist.

There is one aspect of licensure I would like to comment on further. This has to do with licensure of a school that is not under the ministry of a church. I see no reason why the state should license any schools. Schools exist to meet the needs that parents have to educate their children. *Parents, not civil rulers, are responsible for the education of their children.* Therefore, parents should not have to get permission from the state to educate their children. The state has no more right to curb the freedom of the parents than it has to curb the freedom of the church in this matter. There should be *separation of family and state*, just as there is separation of church and state. This means also the *separation of school and state*, for the school is the agent of the family.

Separation of church and state does not mean that the church is to be religious and the state is to be secular. Church and state are both under God. The family is also under the authority of God. Jesus told Pilate that he would have no authority over Him, were it not given to him by God. Paul says that the powers that be are ordained of God. The three basic institutions are family, church, and state. They each have spheres in which they are to operate. They have separate functions, but each is to be under God.

The civil government does not need the permission of the church to execute murderers. The church does not need the permission of the state to proclaim the gospel. The family does not require the permission of church or state to instruct children. When church or state tries to assume the prerogatives of God and control all of society, then we are headed for tyranny. God would have us live in freedom under Christ. Jesus Christ is God. He is Lord. He gives us permission to educate our children. We don't require a license from any civil ruler.

Accreditation

"I believe in God the Father Almighty, Maker of heaven and earth. And in Jesus Christ, His Son. . . ."

These are the familiar words of the Apostles' Creed, known by Christians everywhere. In the Latin from which the creed is translated, the words "I believe" are expressed in one word. That word is "credo." Our word "creed" comes from "credo." The creed is a statement of what we believe.

Some other familiar words have their root in "credo." They are "credit," "creditor," and "accredit." When we say that we believe in God and in Christ, we are saying that we are putting our faith in a higher Being. When a school is accredited, the school is putting its faith in a higher institution which grants the school legitimacy. *When a school is accredited by the state, the school is putting its faith in the state and being accepted by the state.*

Thus, accreditation is a religious act. This explains why accreditation is one of the means used by humanistic governments to control Christian schools.

I have operated a Christian school for over 25 years. In interviews with parents who are considering enrolling children, I have heard one question over and over, "Is the school accredited?"

This is always one of my favorite questions. I was always proud to say, "No, we are not accredited, and we have no desire to be accredited."

These parents had been attracted to the school because we had established a good reputation in the community. Naturally, they were puzzled at my response. Many did not ask the question. Perhaps they just assumed we were accredited.

Why did these parents ask about accreditation? Primarily, I believe, because they have heard repeatedly that good schools are always accredited. Some think that if the school is not accredited, the students will not be accepted if they transfer to the public schools, or that they "won't be able to get into college."

Let's take a look at some of these concerns. Let's start with the "won't be able to get into college" idea. The school I operated has now graduated 18 classes from high school. We have never had a student who couldn't get into college. I wouldn't claim that our graduates always get into the college that is their first choice. But then again, I don't know any school that could make that claim.

One of the most interesting experiences we had was with our first graduate. She was not only our first graduate, she was our only graduate that year. She had barely turned "sweet sixteen" before she was graduated. She was valedictorian (top student) of her high school class, of course. She also ranked last in her class. It depends on how you look at it. Anyway, she enrolled in a branch of the University of Virginia.

The following year, we had twice as many graduates: two. One of them enrolled in the same branch of the University of Virginia. Then the second one applied there. At that point, I got a phone call from the admissions office, "Mr. Thoburn, what are you doing about accreditation?"

"Nothing! Why?" was my quick reply.

"Well, we have an application here from one of your students, and I notice that your school is not accredited," she explained. "We have one of your students here now, and she is doing very well. But we can't take any more. We aren't allowed to take students from non-accredited schools."

I pointed out that the student who was applying had done quite well on the College Entrance Examination. She admitted this was the case, but it didn't matter.

Then I said, "O.K. I won't send any more students your way. (Actually I preferred to see them go to a Christian college anyway.) I'm thinking about starting my own college." I was, too.

This obviously got to her. The next morning I got another call from her. "We took this up with the Dean and the Admissions Committee. We've decided to consider your graduates on an individual basis." (I guess I'm not very bright. I thought all students were considered on an "individual" basis.)

The student was admitted, and every student who applied there since has been admitted. The fun thing about this whole episode was that our first graduate finished her course at this college at the ripe old age of 20, and she was the valedictorian of her college class (numbering over 400 students).

Of course, from their point of view, they also got what they wanted. I never did start a college.

I ran into this "problem" of getting students into college on other occasions, but every time the student was admitted. One family that had a student graduate from another Christian school came to me for help. The United States Army wasn't going to take students from non-accredited schools! We worked that one out rather fast, and the young man got into the service.

Now we are finding that the colleges are actively trying to recruit our students. They want to talk to our seniors. One college president called me. He said they were eager to get students from Christian schools. The service academies regularly contact us for possible students.

If we Christians operate excellent schools, we don't need to worry about our children getting into college. The colleges that are worth attending will appreciate young people who are interested in something other than beer and pot.

I remember visiting prestigious Stanford University at the time of the student riots in the late 1960's. It looked as though it had been bombed out. Broken windows had been boarded up. It was a war zone. The colleges in that era learned to welcome students who weren't going to tear the place apart.

One of my own sons (who now runs our Christian school) was graduated from our high school at age 15. When he went off to college, he took college level entrance tests, and received a full year of college credit. He was a sophomore in college at age 15, and graduated at age 18. One of his complaints about college was that the students were immature.

What about transferring to the public schools? This has to be the biggest bugaboo of all. We have found that our students are often put *ahead a full grade* when they transfer. On the other hand, we often have to put them back a grade or two grades when they transfer to us from the public school.

We need to realize that the government schools want every child they can get their hands on. It means more money and more power for them. They are not going to make it difficult to transfer back to their schools. All they want to do is to create the impression that it is some kind of "problem" so parents don't opt for the Christian schools in the first place.

Is There Any Danger in Accreditation?

If a school feels accreditation is really important to them, I recommend joining with other like-minded schools and having a private accrediting agency. There is danger in getting state accreditation or in being accredited by a private organization that has a humanistic philosophy.

State accreditation involves state control. Furthermore, we should not want humanists passing upon the standards of our schools. The accrediting agency is going to influence (in a subtle manner in many cases) the curriculum, the educational philosophy, teacher qualifications, and other aspects of the school.

The requirements for accreditation may appear to be very reasonable and consistent with the school's standards. The difficulty may arise when the requirements are changed. The new standards may be totally unacceptable. Then the school must accept them or "lose its accreditation." In the public mind, it is a terrible thing for a school to "lose its accreditation." It is better never to have had it in the first place.

Accreditation can work hardships upon a school. In Holland, Michigan, many years ago, the Christian schools were told that they must have shop and home economics to be accredited. The schools wanted neither because they felt this was being handled adequately at home. Requiring such courses can be expensive, not to mention that time is taken away from teaching the basics.

Understand also that these schools were run by Dutch-background churches. (*Holland*, Michigan!) Those people were very often farmers. Their churches were filled with skilled craftsmen. Dutch-owned Michigan manufacturing companies had and still have excellent national reputations for high quality production. These people did not resist the idea of shop courses because they had no respect for craftsmanship. They just knew that students could learn such skills better in the local community in profit-seeking businesses. What students needed to learn in school were the intellectual skills that are normally only available from trained teachers.

Accrediting agencies might require a lower teacher-pupil ratio than is necessary for effective teaching. This would raise the cost of education without enhancing quality. The result would be that some students could not afford to attend the Christian school.

A law school in Northern Virginia was established by Christians. It had Biblical ethics as its basis. The school was refused accreditation by the American Bar Association. As a result, the students couldn't take the bar exam. If they couldn't take the bar exam, they couldn't practice law. Thus a chain of control was set up.

The reason given for not accrediting the law school was that the American Bar Association was opposed to "free-standing" law schools. The law school needed to be merged with a college or university. The school knuckled under and merged with a state university. Needless to say, it is no longer a Christian law school.

I suspected all along that the bar association's real reason for not accrediting the law school was its Christian roots. Not long after this, Oral Roberts University had difficulty getting its law school accredited. The Christian connection was clearly the problem. The American Bar Association backed down when a suit was threatened. (Think of it: lawyers not wanting to go into court! To use a medical analogy, they faced the prospect of having to swallow some of their own medicine.)

Before going on to a related subject, I want to cite another example to show how accreditation is not what it is cracked up to be by the child controllers. A few years ago, a young lady graduated at the top of her high school class in Washington, D.C. She did so poorly on her college boards that she could not get into a local university! Imagine how the other students must have fared. The same thing happened in a Baltimore city school. The valedictorian of a large high school couldn't get into college because of poor college board scores. What a terrible thing to do to students. They and their parents are proud of the education they think is being delivered by accredited schools, and then comes the day of reckoning. What good did that accreditation process do them? It kept them in a dream world.

Certification of Teachers

Mark Twain said that all you need for a school is a teacher sitting on one end of a log and a student on the other end. (A junior college English teacher in California says that her students frequently do not know who Mark Twain was.) Those educationists who are more interested in control than in imparting knowledge would insist that the log be the right length and diameter. They would at least want a license posted in a nearby tree to legitimize such a learning situation.

The teacher on the log would need to be "certified" by the state. He (or she) would be required to attend an accredited college or university and to major in teaching methods. Then the state would issue a license for that person to teach and certify which subjects he could teach.

If Albert Einstein offered to impart some wisdom in the area of physics, the state would say, "We're sorry, Mr. Einstein. We realize you know more about physics than anyone else in the world. But you have not taken the prescribed courses in an accredited college. So you cannot be certified to teach."

Adam Smith never took a course in economics. James Madison never took a course in political science. Karl Marx never studied economics or political science; his doctorate was in philosophy from a university he never actually attended because he wasn't going to be granted a degree from the University of Berlin, where he had been a student for years. (He sent in his doctoral thesis to the University of Jena, and they granted his degree by mail.) Charles Darwin had a master's degree in theology, not biology. John Dewey never suffered the mind-dulling horrors of a university education department.

Who are the accreditationists trying to fool? They couldn't hire the very people whose works are taught in their best schools!

In Virginia a few years ago there was a man with a Ph.D. who was married to a woman with a master's degree in mathematics. They were teaching one of their children at home. The state hauled them into court. The parents won in this case, but many have lost.

You see, it is not enough even that a person have a college degree. He is not considered qualified to teach because he has not had the education courses—just like John Dewey. The Christian school that I direct once employed a man with two earned doctorates, a law degree, and five other earned degrees. Yet he would not have been legally qualified to teach in most public school systems. (Nor would they have hired him anyway; they are required by law and union contract to pay people in terms of the number of degrees they hold. He would have bankrupted the school system!)

One of the ways that governments try to control the Christian schools is by requiring them to have certified teachers. To be certified, the teachers have to sit through four years of dreary "methods" courses in some college approved by the government. In these courses, they are indoctrinated in humanistic philosophy. My wife took such a course. She was fed the secular ideas of our old philosopher "friend," the atheist and socialist John Dewey. (The college she attended, incidentally, was a church-related one, so don't assume that humanism is only in state schools.)

After four years of this stuff, my wife was "certified" to teach. Her first year (in a public school) was almost a disaster. She taught kindergarten in Connecticut. They didn't want anything of substance taught in kindergarten. As a result, the kids were bored and restless by the end of the first semester. I can't imagine a more conscientious teacher than my wife. She had two kindergarten classes at that school, one in the morning and the other in the afternoon. The summer before school started she personally visited every child at his home. She is a superb teacher, but the prescribed program of the government schools just doesn't work.

After one year in the state schools, my wife devoted all her life to Christian education. She found that she had to unlearn everything she learned at college. She has been developing successful curriculum materials ever since.

My wife and I started our own school. We seldom hired teachers who were certified by the government, nor did we follow a curriculum just because it was the fashion of the day. We got results and that is what counts. The parents were pleased, so they patronized ("parentized") the school. In my day, we never put out a brochure on the school. Word-of-mouth advertising by satisfied customers helped build our enrollment. (I must admit, my son has made the school so much money with his direct-mail advertising that I figured we might as well let the free market teach us a profitable lesson.)

One time a parent came to me to enroll a child in our Christian school. She was certified to teach first grade. She said she didn't know how to teach her own child to read, and she wanted me to help her. I thought to myself, "This lady has been through four years of college, specializing in education, and she is asking *me* how to teach her child to read!" After all, I had never taken an education course in my life. I majored in philosophy. (Just like John Dewey and Karl Marx. Oops.)

There is a difference between certification and qualification. Some teachers are qualified to teach and some are not. Just because a teacher is certified by the state does not guarantee that he or she is qualified to teach. Many highly qualified persons can not be certified because they have not been through the programs prescribed by the state. The sad fact is that the education majors in our colleges are the "bottom of the barrel" as far as academic standards are concerned. They score the lowest on the college entrance examinations.

You know the old line: "Those who can, do. Those who can't, teach. Those who can't teach, teach teachers."

The public is becoming more aware of the poor teaching that is going on in the government schools. Pressure is being put on the politicians to require competency tests for teachers. Merit pay for teachers is also being advocated. The teacher unions have fought both ideas, although even they are reluctantly admitting there are serious problems in the profession. Teacher unions have job security as a high priority. Competency tests might weed out some of their members. As for merit pay, by definition only a minority of teachers will qualify. The majority who don't qualify will always outvote the minority in the teacher unions.

Summary

The war against the Christian schools is a continuation of humanism's attack on Christian morality and the family. When they kidnapped most children through the public schools, a few children began to slip out of their control. The humanists have used various methods and strategies to regain at least partial control over private schools.

The parents should make the final decision. They need to consult others for guidance, but in any case, state accreditation gives them no important information, with one exception: it tells them that the school's administration has capitulated before the state. That is negative information, not positive.

If Christian parents want independence from the state, they must pay the price financially. They must also pay the price in terms of the world's so-called honors, such as accreditation and certification of teachers. Parents should not use the state's criteria as screening devices. Our goal is to escape the humanist state, not get it to approve of what we are doing, let alone license what we are doing.

But Christians have academic inferiority complexes. They just cannot seem to believe that Christ's way is better, or that our blueprints are better. They pay the price. They are schizophrenic: they pay to get their children out of the public schools, and then they worry about accreditation. Like the people of Israel in Jeroboam's day, they just aren't sure where to worship.

In summary:

1. The "lowest common denominator" theology is always some variety of man-worship.
2. The political religion of "good citizenship" is humanism's substitute for Christianity.
3. This religion boils down to "obey the state."
4. The humanists took over the "golden calf"—the public school system—that the Puritans had constructed.
5. Today, they use other means to control those Christian schools that are outside the direct control of public education.
6. They require the state to license rival schools.
7. This means the state permits the schools to exist . . . for now, and only on their terms.
8. This may involve licensing church ministries.
9. Christians should defend the idea of the separation of family and state.
10. This means the separation of school and state, for the school is an agency of the family.
11. Another means of control is accreditation.
12. Sometimes this is granted by non-civil institutions.
13. The threat of removing accreditation always hangs over the school.
14. Christian schools should not normally seek accreditation, and never by the state.

15. Graduates of unaccredited high schools can still get into top-flight colleges and universities.

16. Certification of teachers is another threat to private schools.

17. The founders of humanist philosophy themselves could not have taught as state-certified teachers.

8

WE MUST COUNT THE HIDDEN COSTS

For which of you, intending to build a tower, does not sit down first and count the cost, whether he has enough to finish it—lest, after he has laid the foundation, and is not able to finish it, all who see him mock him, saying, "This man began to build and was not able to finish" (Luke 14:28-30).

It is clear that Christians have not counted the costs of public education. The costs of private education are clear: so much money per student per year. The costs of public education are deliberately hidden, so as to make political opposition more difficult. This way, the public will demand more of this "free good."

What Christians need to consider is the system of hidden costs in government education. Only then will we be able to make an accurate judgment of whether we should continue to vote to sustain it, let alone send our nearly defenseless children into it.

The humanists are doing their best to raise the costs of sending children to private schools. Even with the "free" tuition of the public schools, a growing wave of parents are pulling their children out of the public schools. The government cannot compete successfully even by giving away a "free" good. So the humanists are trying to increase the difference between their "free" good and private education. We need to recognize this strategy when we see it, and then fight it.

Removing Tax Exemption

"The power to tax is the power to destroy." This is a well-known truth, articulated over 150 years ago by United States Supreme Court Chief Justice John Marshall. Governments have

107

learned that something they don't approve of can be taxed out of existence. This is the context of Marshall's remark: the State of Maryland was trying to tax an agency of the Federal government. Marshall said this was unconstitutional; the Federal government has greater sovereignty than the State of Maryland.

But what about the sovereignty of God? What about the sovereignty of a rival government, God's church? Should the State of Maryland, or any other civil government, be allowed to tax it? If we say yes, then we are implicitly announcing that we believe in the superior earthly sovereignty of the state to the church.

We think of taxes as a means of raising revenue for the government, but the tax code is frequently used as a means to promote social goals. Promoting one social goal always involves sacrificing someone else's goal. There are no free lunches in life.

Under the Internal Revenue Code, certain organizations can be exempt from Federal income taxes. Among these are schools and churches. We understand how the government can control an institution by taxing it. How are tax-exempt organizations controlled? The government controls them by threatening to take away their tax-exempt status. When that happens, the organization has to pay income taxes on its profit. Contributions to the organization are no longer deductible on the donor's tax return. There are numerous other benefits enjoyed by tax-exempt groups. On the local level the church or school will not have to pay real estate taxes.

A school saves the taxpayers an enormous amount of money. If the cost per pupil in a government school is $3,000 per year, then a 500-student Christian school would save the public $1,500,000 per year. We would like to think the public appreciates this, and that the politicians would do everything they can to encourage such schools. That is not the case, however. The secular humanists who control governments want to control the education of the children. They don't care who pays the bill, just so long as it doesn't come out of their own pockets.

A new way of looking at tax-exemption has come into vogue. Legislators and government bureaucrats call the money that

would have been paid by tax-exempt groups "tax expenditures."
They think the government is *subsidizing* the tax-exempt organiza-
tion. Never mind that a school is saving the taxpayers millions.
Schools are treated as though they were on government welfare.

There are pressures from two sides to take away tax-
exemption. There are those who engage in revenue enhancement
(a fancy name for raising taxes) and see an opportunity to enact
another tax. There are others who want to make it as difficult as
possible to run an alternative school. So they threaten to take
away the tax-exempt status of the school.

Back in August of 1978, a major effort was made by the Internal Revenue Service to do just that. They published Revenue
Procedures in the *Federal Register*, the *daily* 200-page list of all the
new Federal agency administrative laws that supposedly were implied in the statutes of the U.S. (How many Americans know that
there is such a publication, let alone read all that fine print every
day?) These procedures said in effect that all private schools were
guilty of race discrimination until they could prove otherwise.
Racial quotas were established. Scholarships had to be provided
to provide the correct racial mix. The whole business gave the
IRS control over schools and churches.

To make it quite clear that Christian schools were the target,
the law specifically exempted schools formed before 1960, meaning the private "preparatory academies" of the elite that had been
discriminating racially for a century before the civil rights movement of the 1960's. Thus, Christian schools that had spread rapidly
since 1965, because of the increasing awareness on the part of
Christian parents concerning the decline of public education and
the dangers of the religion of humanism, were going to be placed
under a massive bureaucratic tyranny.

Christians were alerted by their newsletter network, and they
organized to resist. Over 135,000 letters of protest were sent to the
IRS—the largest number of protest letters in IRS history. Victory
was assured when pressures were exerted on Congress to curb the
plans of humanists in the Internal Revenue Service.

The point is that the bureaucrats insist that whenever the state "grants" tax exemption to an organization, it must conform to government policies. The U.S. Supreme Court confirmed this doctrine when it removed the tax exemption of Bob Jones University in the early 1980's.

This is why churches must be defended as *tax-immune*, not merely tax-exempt. The civil government has no legal right to tax the church in God's eyes. Tax immunity is a God-given right, meaning legal immunity.

We cannot argue this same immunity for non-church schools, since schools are not equally sovereign to the church, but we should at least recognize the threat when it arises.

Land-Use Laws

"An environmentalist is a person who bought his half-acre last year." That is a joke I heard recently from a long-time employee of our county government. As another person put it, "Some people move into Fairfax County, buy a half-acre of land, and then want to control the property of everyone."

"What is zoning?" my brother-in-law, a farmer in Ohio, asked me several years ago. I grew up in that area. We never heard of zoning. A person owned a piece of land and used it for whatever purpose he wished. We were neighborly, and wouldn't think of harming the property rights of someone else. Besides, if we did, we could wind up in court.

Times have changed. Since 1913, land use laws have made it increasingly difficult to use one's own land. Land is looked upon as belonging not to an individual or family, but to the community. At a recent zoning hearing for a church, I heard the head of a civic association state that the church had "selected our site" for its building. The land was privately owned and under contract to the church. The citizens acted as though the land belonged to them!

Removing the Competition

In 1985, the Christian school which I operate applied for a Special Exception to build a school on 44 acres of land in Fairfax County. The government schools in Fairfax normally put 600 children on 10 acres. We applied for 576 children on our 44 acres. This was not acceptable. We lowered the number to 288. It was still not acceptable.

Our site is very secluded. The nearest house would be 600 feet away through woods. It could not even be seen from the school building. The school would generate considerably less traffic than the houses that could be built on the land. In every way, we showed that the school would have less impact on the neighborhood. Even the reporters from the liberal newspaper *The Washington Post* could not understand why there was any problem with a school on the site.

Nevertheless, the County Board of Supervisors turned it down on a tie vote, virtually along party lines. It was pure politics. No official reason was given. The Supervisors don't need a reason. One of them muttered something about the school not being in "harmony with the Comprehensive Plan." Any time the authorities don't like something, they can always say that it isn't in harmony with the Master Plan.

(What the humanists don't realize is that *they* aren't in harmony with the *real* Master Plan, God's Master Plan! The consequences of their lack of harmony will be eternal. They will be subject to eternal zoning. See Luke 16 and Revelation 20.)

The Fairfax County Office of Comprehensive Planning did everything it could to keep us from using our land for a Christian school. The land has a stream flowing along it for about 3500 feet. Next to it is a broad flood plain. We wanted to clear some land there for a soccer field. We were told that we could not clear that land for a play area because it was an "environmentally sensitive" area. One planner said that if trees were cut along the stream, the temperature of the water would be raised, and trout further down the stream would die. If anyone has ever seen a trout in Fairfax County, he is keeping it a secret. The man's reason was absurd. At any rate, I told him we weren't going to remove any trees along the stream.

The county staff tried to make us build a horse trail along the stream so that the public could use our land. In other words, we could not use our own land, but we had to build a facility to be used free by the public. All I got from Fairfax County was a 50% increase in the tax assessment in one year.

I could write a book about land use laws, and someday I just might do it. Let me share a few more choice items from my own experience. Back in 1964, an ordinance was proposed in Fairfax County that would have required all private schools to keep their land free of insects. No insects! Have they ever turned on a porch light in summer? The only reason given for not adopting the ordinance is that they figured they couldn't enforce it.

Getting the necessary zoning or use permit to use land for a school is only the first step. There are also complex site plans that must be drawn up and certified by professional engineers. These are submitted to the county for review. The review takes months and sometimes more than a year. The applicant pays for the "service."

Writing to Myself

In 1965, I was required to write a letter to myself to obtain a site plan for a school building. I had constructed a building in 1964. The next year I wanted to build on adjoining land. I submitted my site plan. It showed that I would be draining some water onto the land where I had built the previous year. A county bureaucrat explained that I had to obtain permission from the owner in order to do that. I pointed out that I *was* the owner. It said so on the expensive certified site plan that was sitting on his desk.

"That doesn't make any difference," he rejoined. "You must have *written* permission from the owner."

So I wrote a letter:

Dear Mr. Thoburn,

I understand that you own land next door to me and that you would like to drain water onto my land. Having known you all my life, and being convinced you have always had my best interests at heart, I give you permission.

I hope this fine mutual relationship continues as long as we both live.

Sincerely yours,

Robert L. Thoburn

The county bureaucrat took my letter and filed it away without batting an eyelash.

Special Exemptions

Land-use laws are employed around the country to make it difficult to start schools. One must find a suitable location for a school. The land must be priced right. The owner must be willing to sell. After finding the right land at the right price and a willing seller, the school may be turned down because of zoning. Some people are even suggesting that schools be allowed only in commercial zones. The cost would be prohibitive. The environment is hardly conducive to a school.

Government schools are exempted from all this. The state has no problems with land use for its own schools. If it wants a piece of land, it uses the power of eminent domain to take the land. Cost is no problem because the taxpayers are forced to pay for it. Often the government gets its site free. A land developer often "donates" the land. What many persons do not realize is that the developer is practically blackmailed into donating the land. The word for it is "proffers." The developer doesn't have to give the land to the government, but if he doesn't offer it, life can be miserable for him. He just adds on the cost to the price of the houses he is selling. Someone always pays.

When the government buys land or builds, it can tax us to raise the money. Governments also sell bonds. The investors' interest on these bonds is exempt from Federal and state income taxes. Bonds also constitute a mortgage on all the real estate and personal property in the county. The interest rate is very low because it is being subsidized by the taxpayers whose income is taxed and whose taxes are raised in order to make up the difference. A Christian school, on the other hand, must pay market rates for financing.

God has called us to have dominion over the earth. The secular humanists who operate the power state want to have dominion over man. As Christians we need to learn a lot more about land use laws and their real purpose. We must become active in government to repeal these laws. Civil government should be protecting our property instead of confiscating it by zoning laws. Property owners who want to control the land around them should enter into voluntary arrangements with their neighbors. Covenants made in this way will protect property owners from undesirable encroachments.

Fairfax County proposed an ordinance in the 1960's requiring churches to obtain Use Permits in order to build. Only six Christians came to the public hearing to object. This was in a county with a population of nearly one half million.

But times are changing. Recently, Fairfax County proposed to regulate what went on inside the church buildings. The Christian community came out in vast numbers. Over 100 speakers signed up. In the middle of the first speech, the county supervisors ran up the white flag. They were ready to surrender, and did. If the Christians had come to the initial meeting when Use Permits for churches were legislated, the situation today would be different.

The Other Costs: Hidden and Not So Hidden

"Free" public education isn't free. It isn't even cheap. Not by a long shot. For starters, there are the visible costs of operating the schools. These costs are usually publicized and may be the only costs the public hears about. Buildings are another cost. If the money is borrowed, the cost of interest must be figured. Tax-exempt interest-bearing bonds are a hidden cost, as I pointed out previously. No taxes are paid by public schools on their vast real estate holdings.

The money to run the schools is collected by another part of the bureaucracy. That cost must be figured in. All money that comes from the state must be considered. The aid from the Federal government is also a cost. There are many subsidies, such as those for milk and school lunches, that represent a real cost to the taxpayers. There are license fees for buses that are "free" to the public schools.

I will not go into the social costs of public education. The tremendous cost to the taxpayers resulting from drug and alcohol abuse traceable to the humanist education of the public schools is beyond calculation. The cost in increased crime and other social problems (so well documented a century ago in Zachary Montgomery's *Poison Drops in the Federal Senate*) is also difficult to calculate.

Suffice it to say that just as there is no such thing as a free lunch, *there is no such thing as free public schools*. They are much more expensive than we realize. Studies show that they cost two to three times as much as private schools, and that is being conservative about it.

By taking so much of our incomes for the government schools, the state is making it more difficult to afford Christian schools. The Christian faces double taxation. He pays for the public schools. Then he pays again for the education of his own children in a school of his choice. The Roman Catholics have been doing this for a long, long time. They generally have large families and many came to this country as poor immigrants. But they have made the sacrifices to send their children to their own parochial schools. It isn't easy, but it can be done.

In a later chapter, I want to offer some very practical advice on how a Christian can afford to put his children in a Christian school. Right now, I just want you to realize that public schools aren't cheap and they aren't free.

Paying the Price of Liberty

Elsewhere, I have referred to Pastor Everett Sileven's battle against the State of Nebraska to keep open his church's school. He won that fight. Nebraska has had a long history of interfering in private education. The state once passed a law making it illegal for any school, public or private, to teach a modern foreign language to any student who had not completed the eighth grade. In *Meyer v. Nebraska* (1923), the Supreme Court struck down this foolish and oppressive law. (I like the title of a book by Orville Zabel, *God and Caesar in Nebraska*.)

Thanks to our Constitution and a Supreme Court decision rendered in 1925 (*Pierce vs. Society of Sisters*), the right to send our children to a non-public school has been firmly established.

Under political pressure from a vicious secret society, the Ku Klux Klan, the State of Oregon had made private high schools illegal. It was a classic piece of anti-Roman Catholic legislation; in that era, there were virtually no private Christian schools in the United States, except those run by Protestant immigrant groups and Roman Catholics. The Supreme Court said Oregon did not possess the authority to enforce such a law. It has been said, though, that eternal vigilance is the price of liberty. Another true saying is that "When the legislature is in session, our liberties are in danger."

We should appreciate the freedom that yet remains in the United States. We should not take it for granted. Have you heard of any Christian schools in the Soviet Union? I had a visitor from Sweden in 1985. She runs a Christian school with about 24 students. Her school is one of only nine Christian schools in the entire country.

We have the freedom to send our children to a Christian school. I have set forth several of the ways the state tries to control these schools. There is one other important method of control that I want to discuss with you. I will call this "pocketbook control." My mother (who never touched alcoholic beverages in any shape or form) used to say, "Talk is cheap, but it takes money to buy whiskey." As applied to education, her comment means that one has the freedom to send children to a Christian school, but it costs money.

There is no question in my mind that financing Christian schools would not be all that difficult *if we Christians could keep all of our own money that now goes to the public schools.* We are talking about a lot of money. The public school system is far more expensive than most of us realize.

There is no such thing as a free lunch. There is also no such thing as a free education. Someone has to pay for it sooner or later. (Usually it is sooner.) The public schools are not free. They are very expensive. The education of your children and my children has a cost attached to it. The only question is who will pay that cost.

Some will say that education is the responsibility of society in general. They will look to government to pay for the education of their children. The only difficulty is that government has no money of its own. The government only redistributes money which it has first taken from the citizens.

Forcing Your Neighbor to Pay

If you send your kids to the public school, you are in effect forcing your neighbors to pay for their education. Here are some ways in which they are forced to pay the bill:

1. A tax on any real estate which they own.

This includes their land and their house. If they do not pay, the sheriff will auction their property. Do you think Matilda Jones, the 90-year-old widow living next door to you, should be forced out of her house because your kids need an education? If so, I suggest you read everything the Bible has to say about caring for widows and orphans.

In most communities, the bulk of the real estate taxes go for the upkeep of the government schools. When the taxing authorities aren't raising the tax rate, they are raising the assessed value of the homes. Property taxes have been going in only one direction for many years. In case you haven't noticed, that direction is *up*. Older people have finally paid off a 25 or 30 year mortgage on their house. It is now free and clear. Or is it? The tax bill is more than the mortgage payment!

But age isn't the main issue. Avoiding getting into our neighbors' wallets is the issue. The eighth commandment does not say, "Thou shalt not steal, except by majority vote."

2. A tax on the real estate of a landlord.

Perhaps your neighbor doesn't own any real estate. Aunt Matilda, as you affectionately call her, rents her house. So she pays no real estate tax. Her landlord (who is supposedly too rich anyway) pays the taxes. The fact that the landlord is rich doesn't justify theft. God is no respecter of persons. Theft is theft.

Christians are told that God intends to bless them covenant-
ally if they obey him (Deuteronomy 28:1-14). He says that the
wealth of the sinner is stored up for the righteous (Proverbs
13:22). Why, then, do Christians vote for wealth-redistribution
schemes? Because they really want to be taxed when God's Word
comes true, and they become the financially successful members of
society? Or because *they don't believe God and His covenantal promises*?

I think it is the latter. They are unwilling to do what God says
they must do in order to prosper. They are also unwilling to wait
for God to prosper them. They do what thieves do. They grab the
other person's money for their own uses.

Christians who vote yes at school bond elections are violating
God's laws against debt (Deuteronomy 15; Romans 13:8), and
also God's laws against theft.

3. A tax on the real estate of local businesses.

Politicians love to tax businessmen. There are reasons for this.
The businessmen are fewer in number than their customers.
Since everyone has an equal vote, it makes political sense to sock it
to the businessmen. The consumers will respond at the polls with
votes for those political leaders who have kept taxes down by this
means. Another reason the businessmen are targets is that they are
perceived as wealthy anyway. They can stand the higher taxes.

The problem with this is that businessmen must pay for expenses. Taxes for a businessman are no different from any other
costs. The businessman must pay for labor, insurance, repairs,
taxes, etc. If the public deliberately votes to increase business
costs, then fewer businessmen will go into business. Some will go
out of business. Then the government will not be collecting real
estate taxes or any other taxes from them. The public will wind up
with fewer goods and services being offered for sale. Fewer goods
will mean higher prices. They will become poorer. God will not be
mocked.

So when widow Jones goes to the grocery store or the shoe
store, she will eventually pay more because of the higher taxes, or
learn to do without. So widow Jones had better remember God
when she steps into that voting booth.

4. A tax on your neighbor's car.

Matilda Jones, at 90, probably doesn't own a car. Her daughter comes by to take her shopping or to church. The car she drives is taxed. There is a sales tax or titling tax that was paid when she bought it. There was a gross receipts tax paid by the car dealer (passed directly on to the consumer in our county), not to mention numerous other taxes imposed in the process of manufacturing and delivering the car. Matilda's daughter pays gasoline taxes, taxes on the oil, taxes on tires, and taxes on repairs, to mention a few.

The taxes increase the cost of buying and operating the car. Part of these taxes are used to educate your kids.

5. A tax on your neighbor's income.

The humanist educators who run the government schools like to get state aid for education. They like federal aid for education even better. Homeowners are resisting higher property taxes. So the educationists turn to the income tax in order to find more money to maintain the spending programs of the "free" public schools. The costs of education get buried in the larger state and federal budgets. An added advantage to the humanists is that greater control of education is vested in the state and federal governments.

6. Other taxes on your neighbor.

I will not go into detail on all the taxes that one's neighbor is burdened with as a result of public education. If I haven't made my point yet, I doubt whether I ever shall. I shall just mention briefly a few more taxes. Some families get guaranteed government loans for education. Even if repaid, these are an extra burden on the taxpayers. With the recent wave of bank failures, many citizens are beginning to realize that government backing and guarantees are a real cost to the taxpayers.

Government school sites are frequently "donated" by developers. We may applaud the generosity of the developers. Often the "donation" is a payoff to the government to get approval of the development. Fewer developers can afford to build homes for the public. Fewer homes means higher prices for home buyers. This is an example of the hidden cost of the government schools.

Another hidden cost is the tax-exempt interest on the bonds sold to finance construction of new government schools. The interest rate is lower than market rates because the bondholder doesn't have to pay income taxes on the interest. That means that someone else gets hit with a higher tax bill. The government is going to collect a certain sum of money one way or the other.

Selling bonds is a favorite way to get school buildings right away. Citizens forget that the bonds have to be repaid. Often these bonds are not repaid for 30 to 50 years. Because of inflation the bondholders frequently never get paid the true value of the money they loaned. The long-term bonds mean that the next generation is paying for the education of our children.

Summary

There are hidden costs in education. The humanists on the one hand do their best to impose hidden costs on their rivals, the Christian schools. On the other hand, they attempt to hide the hidden costs they impose on the taxpayers for maintaining public education.

Christians have not paid sufficient attention to the moral costs of public education. They certainly have not understood the hidden economic costs. It should be the goal of Christians to assess the true cost of private education compared to public education. When they better understand the true costs involved, they will become less resistant to the moral and religious case against the government school system.

In summary:

1. Christians have not counted the full costs of taxpayer-financed education.

2. The cost is not simply the money paid out to finance these schools.

3. The humanists are trying to increase the costs of private education.

4. Too many parents are avoiding this "free" (zero-tuition) service.

5. Tax-exempt schools are threatened with the removal of their tax-exempt status unless they conform to Federal standards.

6. Politicians argue that such exemption "costs" the public.

7. They are seldom ready to count the economic value of the services supplied by the tax-exempt institution.

8. Land-use laws restrict the spread of churches and Christian schools.

9. The government has exempted its schools (that is, its "churches") from these regulations.

10. There are hidden costs in public education: buildings, bonds, depreciation.

11. The cost per student is two to three times higher than in private schools.

12. There are moral costs of forcing your neighbor to pay.

13. Your neighbor may be seriously injured by taxes.

CONCLUSION

The civil government's legitimate role in education is simple enough: to provide instruction for military officers. The government can legitimately fund military academies. It may also choose to fund and operate specialized schools that train people for government service, but only in those areas specified by the Bible as legitimate functions of the civil government. In short, it may buy a product — educational services — related directly to the enforcement of its God-given assignments.

Nothing else? No college football teams? No compulsory attendance laws? No medical schools? No public schools at all? That is correct.

I will not repeat the arguments in detail. Here is the summary of the Biblical case against public schools.

1. There is no such thing as neutral education.
2. The justification of public education is that it teaches public morality.
3. At the same time, the humanists insist that religion be kept out of public education.
4. This assumes that there can be morality without religion — no ultimate right and wrong that cannot be proved by logic, which in fact is the basis of logic.
5. This assumption is the key myth of public education.
6. Parents are responsible for the education of their own children.
7. Parents retain control of education by paying for it.
8. Any violation of this principle transfers at least some responsibility and sovereignty to the other two governments (church, civil).

9. Any violation of this principle also involves theft by ballot box, leading to an increase in public conflict.

The fact is that today education is mostly taxpayer-supported, and therefore is mostly political. It is entirely religious. Therefore, Christians have a moral obligation to make political war on the public schools. They are the most entrenched enemy of Biblical faith in the United States today. The public schools are "public enemy number one."

Part II
RECONSTRUCTION

9

WHAT THE FAMILY CAN DO

After the death of Moses the servant of the LORD, it came to pass that the LORD spoke to Joshua the son of Nun, Moses' assistant, saying: "Moses My servant is dead. Now therefore, arise, go over this Jordan, you and all this people, to the land which I am giving to them—the children of Israel" (Joshua 1:1-2).

No man shall be able to stand before you all the days of your life: as I was with Moses, so I will be with you. I will not leave you nor forsake you" (Joshua 1:5).

God wanted the Israelites to be future-oriented. They were to go in and possess the land as He had promised. They were to be optimistic. God promised them victory. They were to take over completely the land of Canaan.

God has promised that the meek shall inherit the earth—the meek *before God*. Christians are to occupy until Christ returns (Luke 19:13). To occupy means *to take over*. Paul says that the saints shall judge the angels (1 Corinthians 6:3). Jesus said to go into all the world to preach the gospel and disciple the nations. He requires that we teach them all the things He has commanded us (Matthew 28:18-20). Jesus promises to be with us. We are commissioned to go by Him to whom all authority in heaven and on earth has been given. We are promised victory. We are to be optimistic. We are to be future-oriented. Our duty is to carry out Christian Reconstruction. The earth is the Lord's. We are to claim it for Him.

In the following chapters, I want to set forth some specific things that we need to do as Christians. There are concrete ways in which we can act to advance Christ's kingdom. Faith without works is dead. It is not enough to agree with the teachings of the Bible. We must act in terms of Biblical truths. Let us see what we can do in the field of Christian education.

The first step is to get your children enrolled in a Bible-believing Christian school, or to begin educating them at home.

How to Choose a Christian School

Not very many years ago the problem of choosing a Christian school would have been fairly easy to solve. Most communities had no Christian school. Often there were only one or two schools available from which to choose. Now there are many Christian schools, especially in the suburbs of our large cities. How should a parent choose the right school for his child?

If your church has a Christian school, you will probably decide to enroll your children there. The doctrinal position of the school presents no problems. The cost is probably low. You know the school staff personally. The decision is easy for you. You send the children there.

I have helped start many church-related (parochial) schools. They have many advantages. Besides the personal, doctrinal, and financial benefits of a church-related school, there are a number of administrative benefits. The physical plant is already there. This helps to cut costs and makes getting started easier. An organizational structure is in place. There is a lot of incentive to get the school moving as a "ministry of the church."

But, there are disadvantages to a church-related school. Since such schools are run by the church, they may tend to be exclusively church centered rather than inclusively family centered. The Roman Catholic Church has operated a system of parochial schools for a long time. They are controlled from the top. The Roman Catholic Church is operated on a top-down system of church government. Naturally, their schools are run that way, too. Also, these days liberation theology (baptized Marxism) is beginning to get into Catholic schools. This is deadly wherever it appears—and it is spreading in many Christian institutions, including seminaries.

The family is a separate institution from the church. The church should not take over family functions, any more than it should try to dominate the state. The church is a ministry of grace. It is God's institution on earth to carry on public worship, to proclaim the Gospel, and to carry out the Great Commission. The church is to proclaim the Word of God and apply it in the lives of believers. The church should facilitate parents so they can adequately carry out their responsibility to educate their children, along with other things. The church should also encourage us to fulfil our duty to labor in our vocations, to be involved in civil government, etc.

The minister teaches that the earth should be subdued to the glory of God. The members then carry out that dominion mandate.

Recently, the minister of a large church told me that most of the problems he had in his ministry centered around the Christian school the church is operating. He sees a serious problem with a church-run school. Some church schools have discipline problems because an attempt to deal with problems in the school has repercussions in the church. The admissions policy of the school will probably have to provide for acceptance of any child in the church.

In some church schools all teachers have to belong to the sponsoring congregation. This makes it difficult to get the best-qualified staff.

Perhaps the major disadvantage with a church school is that the school is all too often looked upon primarily as an evangelistic outreach of the church. Evangelism becomes the main thrust of the school. This may hurt the academic progress of the school. Christian children should have the very best education. *The primary purpose of a Christian school should be to train covenant children in all areas of knowledge*. If children come to a saving knowledge of Christ in a Christian school, that is well and good. But the Christian school is not just another way to win the lost.

I mentioned earlier that the availability of a building can be an advantage of a church operated school. This may also be a disadvantage. Usually the Sunday School rooms of a church are quite small. The Christian school classes will have to be small also. Such small classes, while considered an advantage, will increase costs a great deal. A larger class can be taught just as efficiently. The increased income makes it possible to lower tuition costs, to acquire better equipment, and to pay teachers adequately. The church facilities may also lack in other respects also.

One pastor, Morris Sheats in Dallas, has a very productive comment on the structuring of schools which is especially applicable to churches which don't have proper facilities.

He suggests that the parents who want a school form a private corporation and build facilities which the church would then rent from the school at sufficient enough rates to cover the basic cost of the facilities. Then they are responsible for the oversight of the school, and the pastor does not have to take time from normal pastoral duties. The responsibility is placed squarely where it should be: on the parents.

Of course, in choosing a non-church-related school, great care must be taken to insure moral and academic integrity. You *know* your local church. You may not know your local Christian school; so, check them out carefully.

In choosing a school, I would consider the following:

1. The doctrinal position of the school.

As a Christian, I want my children in a school that believes the Bible to be the infallible word of God. The school should subscribe to the fundamental doctrines of the faith. I won't take the space to list all of them, but they would include belief in the sovereignty of God, the Trinity, the virgin birth and resurrection of Christ, the atoning death of Christ on the cross, salvation by grace through faith alone, creation, and the validity of God's law.

2. The educational philosophy of the school.

Just because a school calls itself "Christian" does not make it so. A school may appear to be sound doctrinally and still be teaching humanism. I suggest that parents read R. J. Rushdoony's *The Philosophy of the Christian Curriculum* to become better informed on a Biblical approach to education.

3. Qualifications of the staff.

I would start with the administrator. He or she will be the key person in the school. I would ask enough questions to satisfy myself that the director of the school is a committed Christian who understands what a Biblical approach to education is. I would look at the director's academic background and experience. I would ask what he considers the purpose of the school to be.

I also would ask about the qualifications of the teachers. The statist educator will advise you to ask, "Are your teachers state-certified?" That is an easy question to ask. It also is a poor question. The school administrator could answer, "Yes," and the parent would be satisfied.

It is not that difficult to attend college for four years, get a degree in education, and become certified by the state. Many teachers are certified, but not qualified. You want the best you can get, so don't settle for "certified." Ask enough questions so that you are satisfied. If the school has good teachers, the admissions director will be glad you are asking the questions.

When asking about teachers, don't be afraid to probe. Find out where they went to college, what kind of grades they made, and what other training they have. What books do they read? What do they believe? What kind of results are they getting in the classroom?

Most parents want their children to have experienced teachers. Don't confuse the experience with the number of years someone has been teaching. A member of our local taxpayer's alliance once noted that a teacher may have one year of experience repeated 20 times. Some teachers learn from experience. Others never grow on the job. I have seen young teachers fresh out of college outperform those who have had many years in the classroom. Don't prejudge a teacher just because he or she hasn't been teaching a long time.

In making judgments about teachers, I would find out about the particular field or grade the teacher handles. If he is teaching biology, I would delve into that field. When I was interviewing prospective teachers as a headmaster, I questioned a teacher who had majored in U.S. history. I asked her what she thought of the New Deal. She replied, "Do you mean Nixon's trip to Red China?" I concluded she didn't know much about history. I asked a prospective English teacher to define an adverb for me. She couldn't. Needless to say, I looked elsewhere to find a teacher to fill that position.

4. Visit some classrooms.

The front office may tell you what a fine school they have. Be sure to visit some classrooms to see for yourself. In a few minutes, you can learn much about the school. Is the teacher in control of the class? Is she organized? Is learning going on in the classroom? In the lower grades, we demonstrate what the children are doing in their phonics, reading, arithmetic, penmanship, Bible, etc. Go over to your local government school to visit. Ask them lots of questions, too. Why not? You're paying their salaries.

While you're in the classroom, observe the physical condition of the room. Is there paper all over the floor? I have been to many government schools. Once I had difficulty parking the car because there were so many beer cans and bottles thrown around. A school facility doesn't have to be expensive, but it should be neat. An orderly atmosphere will indicate order and meaning in the school. A junky chaotic situation speaks for itself.

My wife and I were invited to a private school as consultants. On the way from the airport to the school, the headmaster took time to buy a lawnmower. We soon discovered the reason. The grass at the school was at least six inches tall. The school sign was falling down. We learned that the school gave no report cards. The public schools in that community must have really been bad for that school to have enrolled any students.

5. Look at the textbooks.

About 20 years ago I was visiting St. Thomas Episcopal School in Houston, Texas. Some of the teachers attending the conference were upset by the lack of good textbooks for the Christian schools. I recall Headmaster Henry Walters telling us that a good teacher doesn't need textbooks. He was right. An outstanding teacher can manage without textbooks or with poor textbooks. Such teachers are not in plentiful supply at salaries that most Christian schools (meaning parents and supporters) are willing to pay.

Textbooks influence students. When I was a lad in school, I thought everything in print was true. I would have believed the medicine man's pitch when he barked, "Don't take my word for it. Don't take anyone's word for it. Just read what it says on the bottle!"

Since most teachers find textbooks very helpful, a school may as well have the best. Much progress has been made in this area in the past 20 years. We still have a long way to go. When you are sizing up a school, look carefully at the materials the student will use. If the school is using essentially the same humanistic books the public schools use, then you had better find out why.

6. Consider the performance of the students.

Jesus said, "By their fruits you shall know them." This was his test for religious profession. In education, we can look at performance.

Testing is one way to measure performance. The school should send regular reports to the parents. A report card should give specific objective information. I have looked at all kinds of report cards over the years. Many of them tell you practically nothing. I prefer the old-fashioned kind with letter and number grades. Promotion to the next grade should be based on achievement, not how old the child is or how tall or how much he weighs. God requires honesty and we should have honesty in reporting.

God tested Adam and Eve in the Garden of Eden. He tested the Israelites throughout their history. He tested Jesus in the wilderness. Testing is part of the Christian's life. It should not be avoided in the school. When choosing a school, look at test results. Find out how the children do on standardized tests and on the college boards. Always take into account the ability of the students. A school with a very exclusive admissions policy should have better results than one that takes students from almost any background.

7. Talk to your friends and neighbors.

A good source of information is to talk with parents who have children enrolled in the school you are considering. If you don't know any, then ask the school for references.

8. Consider the cost and transportation availability.

9. Don't make a decision based merely on the following:

a. Cost. A school may be very expensive, but not so good.

Many excellent schools are inexpensive. In education especially, you don't always "get what you pay for."

b. Accreditation. The public schools are usually accredited. The mere fact that a school is accredited by someone is no assurance that it is the best school for your child. The same goes for licensure.

c. Nice campus. I have had many a family enroll their children because we had such a "beautiful campus." We Christians should pay attention to architecture, landscaping, and all the rest —but *first things first*. Remember that we worship God in the beauty of holiness, not the holiness of beauty. Man looks on the outward appearance. God looks on the heart. We should think God's thoughts after Him. Look beyond the buildings and grounds. The government schools have spent billions on physical facilities. Remember what Mark Twain said about the teacher on one end of the log and the student on the other.

Paying for Your Children's Education Yourself

I was raised on a farm, close to nature. I have observed that mother cows watch carefully over their calves. I have been confronted more than once with "setting hens" (chickens keeping eggs warm until they hatch) that would put up a tough fight if you tried to disturb their nest. I have seen the killdeer trying to divert attention from her nest of baby birds on a stony hilltop. Parents have a God-given concern for their offspring. This carries over to education. *No one has more interest in the education of a child than a mother or father.* This is the key to financing a Christian education for your child. God teaches us this by His revelation in nature. He also teaches this lesson in His special revelation, the Bible.

I want to suggest specific ways that you can finance a Christian education for your children. Here they are:

1. Include tuition to a Christian school in your budget.

When you set up a budget, you are establishing spending priorities and spending limits. You are making a plan and that plan should include education for your children. Many parents have a plan to send their children to college. They make financial commitments years in advance. Elementary and high school education are just as important as college, if not more so. If your child gets a good foundation, he may win a scholarship to college. If he doesn't get a good foundation, he may never make it to college. Start planning for your children's education even before they are born.

2. Give up something in order to have money for the education of your children.

Sell your television set. Someone gave us a black and white set about 23 years ago. After a few months it went on the blink. We threw it out. We never owned another set until about four years ago. The cost of a TV isn't all that much. The time spent watching TV is the greatest cost. Sell your TV, and then use your time to earn extra money or work with the children on their education.

Drive a secondhand car. The first owner of a car pays the most per mile to drive that car. The second owner pays less, and the third owner even less. It is the most effective means of redistributing wealth in America, and it is all voluntary. One of my sons has a car with over 200,000 miles on it, and it drives like a top. Yes, I just bought a new car. I have purchased several new cars in the past 10 years. However, I was 38 years old before I bought my first new car. For many years we didn't even have a family car. Our Volkswagen Microbus was turned into a school bus. We got around in a pickup truck.

Besides, I only have three children left who are still in need of formal education. The tuition money I don't have to pay for my five now-independent children buys me a new car every year, if I need one.

3. Move to a less expensive house.

When most are house shopping, they usually figure out the highest monthly payment they can afford. Then they buy the most expensive house for which they can qualify. A better plan is to buy an adequate house at a lower price. The difference can be used to finance the education of our children.

The best plan may be to rent rather than to buy. One can rent a house for less than it costs to buy that same house. I own several houses which I rent to others. I'm renting the one I live in. It would cost me twice as much per month to buy. When we started our school, I looked for months for a place to rent. We found a charming brick house on two acres of land. We lived upstairs and held classes downstairs. The rent was $150 per month. (Those two acres today are worth $1,000,000.) The house had 14 foot ceilings. After deducting a portion of the rent for school, we had a nice place to live at low cost.

4. Invest in your children.

Children were the chief economic asset on the American frontier. The Bible says that the man is happy who has his quiver full of them (Psalm 127:5). Children are a heritage from the Lord (Psalm 127:3). What could be a better investment?

When Mrs. Thoburn and I were married, we had practically no money. I was a student in seminary. She even paid for our wedding license because she was afraid I couldn't come up with the three dollar fee. We couldn't afford to get married. We certainly couldn't afford any children. We have eight children nonetheless. As our family grew, we were better off financially. We invested in our children, and it has paid off very well. The payoff goes far beyond monetary considerations.

Children also make people work harder.

We are living in the information age. There is a premium on knowledge. Investing in our children's education is more important than ever. If they have the knowledge of the Lord and an understanding of His creation, they will be prepared to earn a living.

5. Get an extra job.

You probably work 40 hours per week on your regular job. If you can't cut spending in order to finance your children's education, then the only alternative is to increase your income. One way to do that is to take on an extra job. People "moonlight" to buy a boat or to afford a vacation. Why not work some extra hours each week to pay for schooling? There is no law of the Medes and Persians (and certainly none in the Bible) that says we can work only 40 hours per week. I would never have made it financially on 40 hours per week.

The 40-hour work week is the salaried man's trap. It is a mark of present-orientation. It is the mark of a grim retirement. It is "part-time retirement in advance." Avoid it.

6. Perhaps your wife can earn some money.

Your wife should not work outside the home if the result is the neglect of the children. When consideration is given to costs of transportation, clothing, food, taxes, babysitting, etc., the extra income of a working wife may be illusory. A part-time job may work out best. A part-time job at the Christian school may be ideal.

At our school, we employ mothers to drive our buses. We use small buses that can be kept at home. The mothers may bring preschool-age children with them on the bus. Their own enrolled children are with them on the bus. The child's vacation corresponds with the mother's vacation.

Other part-time jobs at the school might be teaching, assisting teachers, secretarial, or custodial work. A mother might handle a full-time position as a teacher, assistant teacher, or secretary.

A mother could work somewhere other than at the school also. She might be able to work right in her home. My oldest son has electronic typesetting equipment. Several miles away a lady works in her home at an IBM word processor. She types the manuscript in her home. Then it is transmitted by phone to my son's machine. Today's technology is opening up all kinds of possibilities for women and men to earn income without leaving their homes and jeopardizing family integrity.

7. Put the children to work.

Several years ago, I was on a trip with a minister. I talked with him about Christian education, and before the trip was over, I had convinced him that his children should be in a Christian school. The difficulty was that he had about eight or nine children and could not afford the cost. I suggested that the children work, and they did. They did custodial work at the school. They distributed flyers door-to-door to advertise a branch school we were starting. Eventually the minister started a Christian school of his own.

My own children have worked at the school from the time they were small. They would start out emptying waste baskets. Then they would vacuum carpets. As they grew older, they mowed the lawns. The child who was 10 days old when the school began now runs the school. At age 23 he was conducting an interview when the parent said, "You are very young to be running a school."

He replied, "I have been working here for 15 years."

What is a child's incentive? In a family-owned school, it can be a lot of incentive, especially when they grow older and learn accounting. You never know when you'll meet a Saudi Arabian — or someone else — who will make you an offer you can't refuse.

Several of our students have worked to pay their own way through school. The student who works has a greater appreciation for the education he is receiving. There are tax advantages, too. The student is in a lower tax bracket than the parents. Under current tax law, a student who works for a school that he attends full-time does not have to pay Social Security taxes.

8. Ask for a discount.

Naturally, you promise to keep your mouth shut about your bargain. The school's owners do not want to face a horde of parents who insist on discounts.

Most schools have some scholarships available. Perhaps they will be able to offer a discount if a full scholarship is not available.

If I have space in the classroom, I would rather have a student sitting there paying half price than to have a vacant seat. The school has certain fixed costs. It is best to have full classrooms.

Perhaps you don't like to ask for a discount. It is better to ask for one than to force your neighbor to pay for your children's education at the public school. At least it is voluntary.

9. Get the grandparents to help.

The grandparents may be barely making it themselves. On the other hand, with their children grown and the house mortgage paid, they may have some extra money. Perhaps you are in line to inherit some money when they die. It might be in everyone's best interest to use some of that wealth to help educate your children. I have known many cases in which the grandparents paid the tuition.

10. Set up a family trust.

You'll need to see your CPA and lawyer about this one. The tax laws are constantly changing, and I am not offering tax advice. I do know that some families set up trusts for their children. As of 1986, the income from the trust goes to the child. Since it is taxed at a lower rate, the benefit is obvious. This device has been used for a long time to provide college education. Problem: the 1987 rules may have abolished this strategy for children under age 14. At any rate, consult your tax experts for the possibilities.

11. What about tuition vouchers?

In recent years, many parents have been working to get a voucher system for schools. The idea is that the Federal government would provide a voucher for each child of school age. The voucher would be worth a stated amount of money. The parents could spend the voucher at the school of their choice, whether public or private. The school would then turn the voucher over to the Federal government for payment.

This idea sounds attractive. The voucher system is supposed to provide more competition among schools. This would lead to improved standards for schools as they compete for the voucher money. The system would give the poor a way to afford private schools. Since the voucher would go to the student and not directly to the school, it is argued that there would be no control over the private schools by the government.

I oppose the voucher system. The present system is unjust, in that parents must pay for the government schools whether or not they choose to use them. The voucher system would be preferable to the present system if that were the only alternative. The voucher system is not the answer. Under the voucher system, the government would still be taking money from some families to give it to others. That is socialism. It is not Biblical.

Can you imagine the red tape that the bureaucrats will wrap the schools in, if this system ever gets popular? It would probably kill off the truly independent schools. Parents would have to pay for public schools, plus voucher-subsidized schools, all under the administrative controls of the Federal bureaucracy. What parents would have money left over to seek out a truly independent, non-voucher Christian school?

While the schools would become more competitive than they are at present, they would not be as competitive as they would under a truly free system. The government would still be supplying the basic subsidy for the schools. The Christian schools would become dependent on these vouchers. If the vouchers were discontinued, the Christian schools would be worse off than before.

A major reason to oppose vouchers is that they will result in further control of the Christian schools by the government. A voucher plan already introduced in Congress provided that the vouchers could be used only in tax-exempt schools. If such controls are already being proposed, there is no reason to think they would not get worse in the course of time.

A better alternative to tuition vouchers would be legislation at the state and local level which would provide property tax relief for any family that did not send its children to a public school.

Suppose Mr. and Mrs. James Smith had a school-age child. Legislation could be passed providing that if the Smiths do not use the local government school, they get $1000 off their real estate taxes. I would not call this government aid, because they are merely being allowed to keep money that the government has no business taking away from them in the first place. The Smith child could be sent to a Christian school, a private school, or educated at home.

This would be a good deal for the taxpayers because the government schools cost a lot more than $1000 per student, especially at the higher grade levels. Legislation such as this could be enacted at the local level without the need to get the Federal government involved. No restrictions would be placed on families as to where or how they educated their children. The tax abatement would be valid as long as they did not send their children to a government school.

12. Figure out ways to cut the cost of education.

Educate your child at home. If you can't do it by yourself, join with another family or a few families. Help one another educate the children in your families. You could provide an excellent education at low cost.

If you prefer a regular Christian school, then figure out ways to keep the costs down. Large classes are more cost effective than small ones. I have all kinds of detailed information in a manual I have published on how schools can operate more efficiently.

13. Pray for God's help and guidance.

God tells us that we have not because we ask not. I have witnessed the providential hand of God many times in the life of our school. The Lord is our shepherd. We shall not want. The government is not our shepherd. We should not look to government to meet our needs. We should look to God.

Summary

It is the family's responsibility to reassert its God-given authority over the education of children. This involves making decisions concerning the kind of education that is needed, and comparing this ideal with the kind of education that is available.

It also involves reaching into the wallet and paying for the service desired. There is no other way. Any attempt to get someone else to pay for your children's education is to abandon a degree of sovereignty over their education. To require others to pay for your children's education is to invite ruthless, power-hungry people to capture the education system. This involves giving up authority over the future. It should be avoided at all costs by Christians.

10

WHAT THE CHURCH CAN DO

But if anyone does not provide for his own, and especially for those of his household, he has denied the faith and is worse than an unbeliever (1 Timothy 5:8).

The church should begin to examine members who are sending their children into public schools. Pressure should be placed on them by the elders. This would include discussions, loaning them a copy of this book or the books by R. J. Rushdoony on education, and similar materials. If a church has a two-tiered membership structure which acknowledges the difference between communicant members (such as children) and voting members, then it should limit voting members to those who refuse to send their dependent children to public schools.

Clearly, no elder or deacon in such a church should send his children into the public schools. It would set a very poor example.

The elders should begin to search out local Christian schools and examine their curriculum materials. The church can recommend schools to members. This is a legitimate service of the church, for the church is the protector of families. It is simply providing specialized information that members may not possess. The pastor should have far more experience in evaluating Christian education than the average member. If not, it is time to find a new pastor.

But what if the local Christian schools are inferior? What is the church's role as protector of families? Is it time for the church to start a school? After all, you can't beat something with nothing.

143

It does no good to criticize the humanist public schools if there is no Christian alternative.

Even better, encourage someone in the local community to start a school. Stand behind him. Give him advice. Get church members behind the project. The church should serve as a motivator. Fear is a major problem. People do not know where to begin. Here is where.

Starting a Christian School

I have written a comprehensive manual on this subject. It has 20 chapters on every aspect of starting a Christian school. There are chapters on organization, finance, buildings, transportation, curriculum, report cards, advertising, scheduling classes, accounting, taxes (not a problem with church schools), teachers, etc. All the basic information is there. We have a starter kit available for those who want to start a Christian school. We have been in the business for 25 years. We run our school as a private, profit-making business. Whether a school is considered a business or not, at least it should be run in a business-like manner.

There are several organizations that provide help in starting schools. There are books, tapes, seminars, and conferences that deal with every aspect of Christian schools.

Organizational Structure

You don't need a big organization to start a school. You might find the job simpler if you just do it yourself. You don't need a board of directors unless you incorporate. You can start a school as a sole proprietor. Another possibility is to join with another person and have a partnership. Schools lend themselves very well to family partnerships.

Another way to organize is to incorporate. You can set up a profit-making corporation or a tax-exempt (non-profit) corporation. See your lawyer or accountant for details. You don't need a lot of people to incorporate.

The church-run school is common. I recommend that the school be kept separate from the church.

Money

You don't need a lot of money to start a school. We didn't have $150 a month for rent when we started in the early 1960's. Three families paid tuition six months in advance to provide rent money. When the realtor asked for an additional $150 for a security deposit, I convinced him to let us pay it in two monthly installments.

We rented an old house, lived upstairs, and had classes downstairs. We started with 32 students and went to 40 the first year. My wife and I taught kindergarten through eighth grade in a two-room school. We doubled our enrollment the second year, and added two teachers. We doubled again the third year, renting another house. We bought land, built four classrooms, and expanded again. The next year we bought more land and built ten classrooms.

We made a profit the very first year. We kept the overhead low, worked our heads off, and provided quality education. By the way, we had five children of our own when we started (ranging in age from five down to 10 days). We subsequently added three more. We had the motivation to run a good school. We were told by a minister that "it couldn't be done." My wife said we were going to do it anyway.

If you need money, form a partnership with someone who has money. He invests money and you invest your time and talent. Both of you should benefit. Do a good job and the marketplace will provide the money to fund expansion. But as in any partnership, always include a buy-out clause. A dissatisfied partner should have the right to buy the school. The contract should allow one partner to make an offer, with (say) 60 days for the other partner to match it. If he does, he then becomes the owner. This keeps the offers honest.

Building

Rent an existing building. Rent space at your church or from another church. We wanted to start a branch in an adjoining county. We spotted a church with a gravel parking lot. We figured they could use some extra funds. They were glad to rent to us. They were a mainline Protestant church, not particularly interested in the Christian school movement, but they liked us as tenants. We paid them so much per student per month. We also paid for any additional utility costs. It was a good deal for them and us.

We sold our original campus property in 1984 because the Saudi Arabian Embassy made us "an offer we couldn't refuse." Now we are renting space in two churches while we are waiting to build our new campus.

And, just to remind you, as a sole proprietorship, my family kept the capitalized value of the land and buildings, not a non-profit school board. Incentives work. Money talks — loud and clear. The non-profit mentality is what gets people to believe other non-profit people when they warn, "It can't be done."

Let me give you an example of capitalization. If you make a profit of a hundred dollars per student per year, after deducting all expenses (including your salary as a manager), and you have 250 students, you have made a $25,000 profit. Now, if long-term interest rates are at 10 percent, what would it cost to earn $25,000? Divide $25,000 by .10. You get a figure of $250,000. If a buyer with this kind of capital to invest considers the prospects of your school to be good, so that he expects to keep making $25,000 a year, and he also expects long-term interest rates to remain at 10 percent or less, he will be willing to pay you close to $250,000 for the whole operation. Capitalization is a most pleasant phenomenon to those who can turn a profit. It encourages people to do things that "can't be done."

Another possibility is to rent or purchase a public school building. We helped to start a school in Washington, D.C. The school was sponsored by a church, and used the church facilities at first. Some members of the congregation opposed the school. Government authorities were uncooperative, too. The pastor and his family decided to start a private Christian school. They are buying a public school building two blocks outside the District of Columbia. They got a bargain. I like to see surplus government school buildings put to such good use. God told the Israelites that

they would inherit wells which they had not dug. The schools being built by the government can and should be privatized. The
meek shall inherit these buildings and turn them into centers of
Christian learning.

Get yourself a financial partner if possible. He can put up the
money for a building and lease it to you. He gets tax benefits, a
monetary return on his investment, and the satisfaction of seeing
the kingdom of God advanced. You get a modern, efficient building in which to run a school. I explain in my manual how to build
so that the school will be profitable. (I'll give you a hint. Don't
build with small classrooms.)

Teachers

Hiring the right teachers is really important. You may have
an excellent curriculum, a handsome building, and plenty of stu
dents, but if you don't have a good staff, you are not going to get
the job done.

Let's start with the director of the school. The title may be
"principal," "headmaster," "director," or whatever. The person who
manages the school is the key employee. You may be that person,
or you may select someone else. The director of the school should
be committed to the Christian school philosophy. He should be
able to organize and be an effective executive. The most important duty of the director is to hire competent staff. The director
does not need to have a degree in school administration.

If the school is controlled by a board, the most important decision they will make is hiring the director. The director should be
competent and should be adequately paid. A skillful manager will
earn his salary by running the school in a professional and busi-
nesslike manner.

There is a rule known as the 80-20 rule. It says that 80% of
your orders in a business will come from 20% of your customers.
Also 80% of your profits will come from 20% of your products. It
is my experience that 80% of your problems in a school will stem
from 20% of your students, and 80% of your problems with teachers will come from 20% of the teachers. The lesson to be learned is
to make the correct decisions in hiring.

In past years, we had a teacher surplus. Now a teacher short-age is developing. But never forget, the word "shortage" should never be used without keeping this qualifier in the back of your mind: "at some price."

I have always found that there are plenty of teachers around. Teachers often prefer a Christian school because working condi-tions are so much better. The pay may not match the public school, but there are other considerations. Semi-retired or retired persons may be good prospects for teaching in a Christian school. The teachers don't all have to be full-time employees. Many mothers are qualified and willing to teach or assist with the school, but are able to work only half a day.

Labor costs constitute the largest item in the school budget. Over the years, we have tried to keep such costs at 45-50% of the total budget. Most schools probably find a larger percentage going for staff salaries.

I learned many years ago that high salaries for employees, low costs to the consumers, and high profits to the owners go together. This is true in a free market situation. I have found that a Chris-tian school can operate this way. We have been able to pay high salaries (especially by private school standards), while keeping our tuition fees modest. At the same time, we have realized a good profit.

Too many Christian schools pay teachers less than they should. The teachers should not be expected to subsidize the school. It is the responsibility of the parents to pay for the cost of educating their children. Many retired Roman Catholic nuns are on government welfare now because they worked for extremely low wages as teachers in parochial schools, and adequate provi-sion for their retirement was not made. This is a shame to the Church.

A prevalent attitude among many Christian schools is that teachers will be "more dedicated" if they are paid less. I disagree with this policy. Teachers should be paid according to the market. Unfortunately, the presence of government in education means that we do not have a completely free market. If we had a truly free market in education, Christian school teachers would be paid considerably more, but they would have to perform far more efficiently.

How can we pay our Christian school teachers higher salaries in the present situation? The answer lies in becoming more productive. It is fashionable in public school circles to blame declining educational standards and poor discipline on large classes. The educational establishment has lobbied for more money to provide smaller pupil-teacher ratios. The fact is that pupil-teacher ratios have been getting smaller in this country, while standards were declining. A prestigious report out of Harvard University several years ago concluded that students in large classes do just as well if not better than those in small classes.

Many Christian schools have the same erroneous notion about pupil-teacher ratios. Some even boast about the small classes they have. Such schools will have to do one of two things. Either their tuition will be quite high, or they will pay very low salaries. If the salaries are high and the tuition is low, the money will have to come from contributions.

It is greater productivity that has lowered costs and improved living standards in our economy. More efficient ways need to be developed to teach children. Lowering the pupil-teacher ratio is going in the opposite direction of greater efficiency and productivity.

Transportation

My advice to someone starting a school is to avoid transporting the students, if possible. I have a chapter in my manual on starting schools that deals solely with transportation matters. Transportation is expensive and occupies much of the attention and time of an administrator.

Curriculum

Detailed curriculum is beyond the scope of this book. I have 38 pages in my manual on curriculum. There are plenty of books and materials available from different organizations that are active in developing Christian schools.

I would stick to the basics in starting a new school. Teach the subjects that every student needs. Don't spread yourself too thin.

Some Additional Thoughts

Don't start your school with any more grades than you need. If your goal is to provide schooling for your own children and they are in the lower elementary grades, then start with those grades. If there is demand from other Christians to add grades, then add them.

As to setting tuition fees, I advise that you follow the guidance of the market. You will not go wrong if you follow the market. If people will pay more, then charge more. If they can't pay what you are charging, then lower the tuition. Pricing is very important. Some areas of the country can support higher tuition. This is generally offset by higher land and building costs as well as higher labor costs. It all tends to even out.

I believe that Christian schools can be started anywhere. We must be flexible. We need to adapt to the community and situation in which we are located. I know a lady who runs a very successful Christian school way out in the country. She doesn't have a college degree. It would appear that she could not run a school and that there isn't much of a market there.

Stay away from a lot of extra-curricular activities. These are expensive and drain a lot of time and energy. The public schools claim to be educating "the whole child." They think it is their responsibility not only to educate, but to take care of social relationships, recreation, etc. They are even providing breakfast in some schools. Such activities further undermine the family. There are always families who will be happy to have you bear the burden of rearing their children. Don't get sidetracked.

Summary

The church is the protector of its families. This means that the church must see to it that every family is encouraged and pressured to get their children out of public schools and into Christian schools, including home schools.

The church should start a Christian school as a last resort. It should cooperate with independent Christian schools locally. It should even be willing to help a congregation member start a Christian school.

The church must protect. If it needs to set up scholarship funds for students, then that is legitimate. But the closer the school is to full parent control, the less likely the lines of responsibility, accountability, and authority will be blurred.

11

WHAT THE CIVIL GOVERNMENT CAN DO

> I will not drive them out from before you in one year, lest the
> land become desolate and the beast of the field become too numerous
> for you. Little by little I will drive them out from before you, until
> you have increased, and you inherit the land (Exodus 23:29-30).

God commanded Joshua to lead the Israelites into the Promised Land. This required them to drive the Canaanites out of the
Promised Land. It was to be a military operation, but not an
overnight military operation.

I think this is our long-term goal with respect to taxpayer-
financed education in the Promised Land. It is to be conducted
peacefully. It is to be conducted as a long-term political operation.
It will have to be organized as carefully as a military campaign.

How are we going to abolish the public schools? The same
way the Israelites conquered the Canaanites: little by little.

Public education is inherently humanistic, for it requires all
people to finance it, and therefore the courts require that it be
structured in terms of the principle of the lowest common religious denominator. It must be built on "common ground" religious
principles. But there are none in principle, and as time unfolds,
any seeming common ground in religion and philosophy becomes
less and less believable, since each group becomes more consistent
with its own religious presuppositions. These presuppositions are
in conflict.

I imagine every Christian would agree that we need to remove
the humanism from the public schools. There is only one way to
accomplish this: to abolish the public schools. We need to get the

government out of the education business. According to the Bible, education is a parental responsibility. It is not the place of government to be running a school system.

We should not waste time trying to improve the public schools merely for the sake of improving them. God didn't tell Joshua to reform the way the Canaanites were living in the land. God wanted no compromise. We should not compromise either. To use a popular modern term, the schools need to be "privatized."

Maybe this sounds like a pipe dream to you. I would simply point out that the majority of the Israelites opposed going in to possess the land. At an earlier period, when the spies brought back their majority report about the "giants" who inhabited the land, the people were afraid. They rejected the minority report which urged them to obey God (Numbers 13-14). The result was 40 years of wandering in the wilderness. When they finally decided to go in to possess the land, God gave them victory.

The intrusion of civil government into education did not take place overnight. I do not think we Christians can close down the government school system overnight either. That must be our goal. We must convince ourselves first. Then we will be in a position to convince others.

Christians need to go on the offensive. The United Methodist Church considered removing the song "Onward, Christian Soldiers" from their church hymnal in 1986. They thought that the song was too militaristic. That church was captured long ago by theological liberalism. We can understand their dislike of the song, even if we don't agree with their theology. The song points to the victory of Christ's church on the earth. They don't want Christians marching. Sadly, fundamental Christians sing the song, but "eat, meet, and retreat" in practice. What is amazing is not that a bunch of liberal Methodists wanted to get rid of it. What is amazing is that pietistic fundamentalists still sing it; it is totally at odds with their view of the impossibility of the earthly progress of the church prior to the second coming of Christ. The song is correct; the pietists are incorrect. It is time that we go forward to possess the land.

Pulling Out of the Slave System

Why do we allow the secular humanists to use our money to indoctrinate our own children while at the same time these humanists make it more and more difficult for us to operate Christian schools? It doesn't make sense. For too long we have been on the defensive. We have been eating the crumbs from the humanists' table and expressing thanks that we can survive. It is time to get out from under.

We could try to take over all the local and state governments, along with the Federal government. We might just take over one state or one county, and then stop funding the public schools. That would be easier to do, but it wouldn't get very far. The whole thing would be declared unconstitutional as long as the remainder of the country was controlled by humanists. Thus, our long-term strategy in almost every political area must be that of full-time salami-slicing. Piece by piece, we will cut back on government expenditures. At the same time, piece by piece, we must build up *Christian institutional alternatives*. You don't beat something with nothing.

I am in favor of any and every effort on the part of Christians to influence and control civil governments at every level. We need to conform civil government to Biblical standards and should offer no apologies for doing so. That is our ultimate goal. As long as education remains under the control of humanists, we have an uphill battle in taking over control of the government. I have campaigned for public office in many a public school, and I can tell you the hostility to Biblical ideas is evident.

What then can we do? Are there any steps we are able to take that will bear fruit? Yes. The most urgent action we can take is to obey God. *We should stop tithing our children to Caesar.* We should notify the public schools that as of today we are withdrawing our children, and that we never ever intend to send them back. Period. No compromises, no qualifications, no deals. They do not get our children back unless they come into our homes and kidnap them — and if they do that, they will face the wrath of almighty God, as well as the wrath of a growing political force in this nation. They may not consciously fear the wrath of God, but they fear the wrath of the mailing list and the satellite television or radio station.

Can you imagine the shock to the humanists if every Christian child in America were withdrawn from the public school system?

It is unlikely that all the Christians will take this kind of action. Like the Israelites, many have fallen in love with the "leeks and onions" in Egypt. All too many will continue to come up with the usual lame excuses for sending the kids off to eat the husks of humanism at the government school instead of feasting with Jesus and His people. It all boils down to the same pocketbook issue: tuition. We agree that government schools would be dealt a devastating blow if all Christians were to remove their children, but we can't get "those other Christians" to act in concert with us. Yet.

So what can those of us do who understand God's requirements in this area? We don't need to wait around for others. We can go right ahead and obey God. Today we can remove our children from the government school and enroll them in a Christian school.

That is the first step. A minority of Christians must continue to show our opponents that we mean business politically. We show them by paying for our own children's education. We first put our *after-tax, after-tithe money* where our mouths are.

Our Opponents Are Increasingly Vulnerable

The government schools are plagued with problems of their own. In 1986, teachers in Texas were complaining because the state was forcing them to take competency tests. At least 10% were expected to fail, and unless they could pass the test in the future, they would lose their jobs. (As it turned out, very few failed.)

At the same time that Texas in effect was admitting that thousands of its government school teachers were incompetent, the state was also trying to take control of the private schools. The Texas Board of Education was being asked to promulgate rules that would severely restrict parents and private schools in their efforts to teach children.

A similar power grab was attempted in Virginia in 1979, when the State Board of Education voted overwhelmingly to request the Virginia General Assembly to give the State Board the power to identify and approve all non-public schools in Virginia. The Board of Education wanted the authority to grant this approval based on rules, regulations, and other criteria that it would promulgate from time to time. Talk about a blank check! Just sign here on the dotted line, General Assembly.

Christians in Virginia pressured the legislature to defeat that power move decisively. The Board passed its resolution in June. By December (before the legislature went into session), they had rescinded their own resolution. Christians defeated them by lobbying the legislators and by putting the legislators on public record. It was an election year, and thus great timing for us. Petitions were the most effective weapon we used. In the petitions, we attacked the public school system and called on the General Assembly and the Governor to reaffirm Virginia's long tradition of educational freedom.

In Texas, a mass rally by Christians was held in the state capital in 1986 within a few days of the school board's almost invisible public announcement of hearings concerning the board's assertion of control over private schools, an authority never granted by the state legislature. This overnight mobilization took place in large part due to a series of radio broadcasts by Christians, especially Marlin Maddoux's satellite broadcast, "Point of View." He had been tipped off about the announcement of public hearings, and he shocked the school board by calling forth thousands of Christians who tried to get in to be heard.

Another Texas radio personality, George Grant, the author of the Biblical Blueprints book on private welfare (*In the Shadow of Plenty*), immediately produced a follow-up tape recorded radio message that warned Christians in Texas of this tyrannical move by the State Board of Education. This message was so effective that word of it got to an out-of-state leader of a nationally known Protestant youth ministry that is involved in producing home school materials, but also involved in selling out the home school movement to state education boards around the nation. He frantically called the directors of Christian radio stations all over Texas, begging them to refuse to broadcast this "dangerous, heretical" message by Grant. I am happy to say that most of them ignored this leader's fear-driven advice. A few capitulated, however.

This leader is terrified of the coming inescapable basic conflicts with humanists in the field of Christian education. He is not alone in his fear of the state or his willingness to compromise for the sake of a little more time and some temporary peace. His view of time teaches him that the church will inevitably lose in its attempt to defeat Satan's forces. His theology says that there is no hope until Jesus comes and "raptures" His people out of trouble just before things get terrible on earth. He has no faith in the church; therefore, he recommends capitulation before the state. He is trying to buy time until Jesus comes and physically delivers us from our earthly problems, since we are incapable of solving them through His grace and by His law. Such views have been dominant in American fundamentalism for over a century.

Bible-believing American Christians have been on the defensive intellectually for a century, and especially since the famous Scopes "monkey" trial in 1925. From then until about 1965, they spent most of their intellectual time running from the humanists or granting humanists many of their presuppositions concerning Biblical interpretation, especially of the first eleven chapters of Genesis. They gave the humanists a free ride. Or more to the point, they allowed the humanists to kidnap their children, pick their pockets, and send them to the back of the bus—in this case, the public school bus. At long last, this is beginning to change. This little book may speed up Christian resistance.

Humanists aren't used to being put on the defensive. They have been having their God-hating way for a long time. God's people have been "eating, meeting, and retreating." Our religion has been escapist in nature. We have been satisfied to worship on Sunday, have prayer meeting on Wednesday, choir practice on Thursday, and some personal witnessing at other times. But we haven't challenged the humanists on their own turf. We've been rather quiet. We've been hiding in the woodwork somewhere.

Now we're coming out and that really gets their attention.

We had better get out of our corner and join the battle. The Bible says that one shall chase a thousand (Joshua 23:10). The Israelites went in to conquer the land. They drove out the inhabitants. Well, they drove out most of them. In a few cases, they lost heart, which is why there is a Book of Judges. The tribes that were left gave them plenty of trouble.

Jesus said, "on this rock I will build My church, and the gates of Hades shall not prevail against it" (Matthew 16:18). The Greek word translated "prevail" means that it is the church that is on the offensive and the forces of hell will not be able to hold their ground. Jesus did not say, "My church will prevail against the gates of hell." Too many Christians act as though He did. It is not the church that is on the defensive; it is Satan's kingdom of hell.

Defensive Political Skirmishes

There are several steps that without qualification all Christians should take politically with respect to public schools.

First, Christians must register to vote. No exceptions, no excuses. Register to vote. Exercise your God-given authority as a judge.

Second, always go to the polls to vote in bond elections. Few people do, and these people tend to be those who are going to be subsidized by the money the bond issue raises if it passes.

Third, without exception, vote no on the bonds. This is doubly God-fearing: it reduces the growth of government debt, and it hampers the public school system.

Fourth, mobilize others to go to the polls to vote against school bond issues. Church members who know what God requires should be warned in advance about the election, and then reminded on the day of the vote to get to the polls.

Fifth, protest in writing all attempts by the politicians to increase property tax rates or the assessed value of property. Vote for politicians who promise (and vote for) property tax relief.

Sixth, attend any meeting of the local zoning commission when a vote to permit the construction of churches or Christian schools is scheduled. Make a show of force.

Seventh, write your local state representative. Encourage him to help balance the budget. Suggest the possibility that if it's really an emergency, the state should hike tuitions at state colleges and universities. What constitutes an emergency? Any suggestion that taxes need to be hiked or that the state budget deficit needs to be increased by the sale of more bonds.

Taking Over Locally

Christians should run for the school board. This may sound like strange advice. After all, I have said that Christians should have nothing to do with the public schools. What I meant was that Christians should not allow their children to have anything to do with public schools. This does *not* mean that we should have nothing to do with them. As I have already said, we should have *lots* to do with them during school bond elections.

Our goal is not to make the schools better, except as a side-effect of making them physically safer (a legitimate function of civil government) and less expensive to the taxpayers. The goal is to hamper them, so that they cannot grow — grow in evil (drugs, promiscuity, abortion advice, etc.), grow in expense, and (if possible) grow in enrollment. Never lose sight of this long-range goal. Our goal as God-fearing, uncompromised, "tuition money where our mouths are" Christians is *to shut down the public schools*, not in some revolutionary way, but step by step, school by school, district by district, as we offer better-quality education to the public.

When a majority of the voters have their children out of the public schools, they will stop voting to support the system. They will "vote their pocketbooks." They will vote no on all school bond issues. They will at last abandon paying taxes to the only established church in America.

Termite Tactics

Run on a platform of increasing school efficiency. This means cost-cutting.

If elected, you must be an instant nice guy, even if you are normally a hard-nosed sort of person. You must be incredibly affable and friendly to other board members. Invite them out for coffee, or to a nice evening somewhere at your expense. You will need "good guy" votes when you start gently pressing for a strategy of temporary reform.

Your personal goal is to convince the middle-of-the-road board members (who always have the majority) that you are not crazy. You are principled, of course, but not crazy. You are not a Bible-toting tyrant. In short, *you are not to be perceived as a loaded loose cannon rattling around on the deck.* This is fundamental to victory in the meetings. It is basic to your re-election, too. *This is a long-term political project.* Your goal must not be to make a fuss for the sake of making a fuss.

A general rule is to avoid at almost all costs any direct, personal confrontations with middle-of-the-road fellow board members. Only if there is some hard-line ideological leftist on the board should you get into struggles. Keep your mouth closed most of the time. Be sweet reason incarnate.

When the board proposes something you don't want, try to avoid a head-on collision. Instead, ask questions, raise doubts, appear confused and tentative about the public's potential reaction, request a study by the school's lawyer, suggest further study of the results of similar decisions by other school systems, but always do your best to avoid confrontations. Make your opponent on the board appear to be the unreasonable one on any issue. Never be perceived by your colleagues as a grand-stander. Let the other guy who voted with you get the credit in the newspaper if it is a popular decision.

Whenever you vote against the others, always plead conscience or caution or ignorance, but don't try to impose your conscience on them. That way, you're perceived as just a nice guy with a weird conscience, or with a legitimate sense of caution.

In short, be as wise as a serpent and as harmless as a dove. You can't destroy the public school system by yourself, so don't try. You can do your best to gum up the system with a smile on your face. Remember, you really are doing the public a service by cutting waste and helping to keep taxes lower.

Your goal must be to sink the ship with the step-by-step cooperation of its captain, crew, and passengers. You must bore many small holes to do this. These holes must be perceived as beneficial to the ship. If you get thrown overboard early in the cruise, you will not succeed in your assignment. Never lose sight of this goal.

Specific Recommendations

First, start pushing for larger classes and fewer teachers. Nudge the board in the direction of refusing to rehire as many untenured teachers as possible. As I have pointed out earlier, a higher pupil-to-teacher ratio cannot be shown to affect student performance. There is little or no statistical evidence showing that lowering the student-teacher ratio will increase student performance. The idea that such a relationship exists is called into question by two generations of shrinking classes and falling student test scores.

The eight-grade little red schoolhouses of rural America and the crowded classes of the New York and Boston public schools turned farm children and non-English speaking immigrant children into the most productive work force in history. They mastered at least the Sixth McGuffey Reader. Today's high school graduates haven't been given equal skills.

Let me give you an example about student-teacher ratios. Wayne Roy was for over three decades a very popular, highly successful social studies teacher in a southern California high school district. One year, he taught the editor of the Biblical Blueprints Series. (His wife taught the children of California governor Dukmejian.) He was a fundamentalist Christian who taught creationism in the classroom, as well as Biblical monogamy, and got away with it, decade after decade. He drove liberals and humanists to despair. They finally gave up trying to get him fired. He took early retirement in the summer of 1986 in order to devote full time as a European tour guide for graduating high schoolers, and to continue his work as a California real estate developer.

He once offered the following deal to the district. Let him teach every senior the required senior problems course. Fire the other civics teachers, or reassign them to other schools or courses. Hire two part-time instructors to read the true & false portions of the exams, and he would read the papers (required for A and B students) and the essay portions of the exams. Double his salary. Save tens of thousands of dollars every year! The district refused. They could have replaced the other high-paid civics instructors, paid him and the part-timers, and pocketed the difference. I think they feared that he could pull it off, so they did not allow the experiment to go forward.

Lesson: you can get more students in those classrooms if the teachers are competent. Why hire incompetent teachers?

Second, personally investigate the curriculum. Get a list of every textbook in use. Use the services of Mel and Norma Gabler in Longview, Texas to help spot really bad public school textbooks. They are authors of the book, *What Are They Teaching Our Children?* ($5.95). You need to read this. Order from:

Educational Research Associates
P.O. Box 7518
Longview, Texas 75607

They also publish a six-page rating sheet of some of the most popular public school textbooks over the past decade. The price is $10. You will also receive their 50-page handbook describing the typical materials they have on hand.

(Discounts on their books are available to parent groups. Such groups can purchase a box of 48 copies of *What Are They Teaching Our Children?* for $72, a very good deal. These books can be used in election campaigns for school board.)

Demand that teachers and principals produce all public documentation handed out during any district-financed trips to professional meetings that would lead to changes in the local curriculum. The board needs to be given full written reports from all those who attend taxpayer-financed meetings of any kind. See if these people can write a coherent sentence.

This may not get the information you need, but if they have to produce detailed reports, they may decide not to go to so many meetings. This helps defend your local school system against national "change agents."

Third, imitate Texas. Get the Board to pass a local "no pass—no play" rule for sports. Make it apply to all extra-curricular activities. The public's education money should not be spent on circuses that are performed by students who are flunking their courses. It cheats the taxpayers, and it surely cheats the athletes, who are being encouraged by their coaches and cheering fellow students to short-change their futures for the sake of a letterman's jacket. It is a terrible trade.

Fourth, always protest when the high school principal is about to fire a coach just because the coach has produced some losing teams. Defend the coach if he has done a decent job teaching his physical education classes to the average student. Teaching PE is legally and officially why he is on the school payroll, not to win after-school games. It is wrong to take money from taxpayers for one purpose (teaching PE) when in fact the money is being used for another purpose (winning games). The issue is *quality education*, not winning teams. If the hometown folks want winning teams, use ticket revenues to hire coaches who produce winning teams. Don't use tax money to subsidize them. Besides, there is nothing like a losing sports record to cool the vocal minority of sports fanatics' support of the local high school. (They want other taxpayers to subsidize their entertainment.)

Fifth, do whatever you can to keep alive the question of student safety. If there are rumors of drugs on campus—if!!!—then encourage the school board to do everything possible to cooperate with law-enforcement officers. This is priority one. First, it is a legitimate task of civil government to enforce safety laws, and drug laws are safety laws. Second, keep a spotlight on the school. If things are bad, the public deserves to know. Christians on the school board should become the defenders of decency, the supporters of student safety. Keep reminding parents how bad things are becoming in the public schools, if things really are getting worse. Never become an accomplice of public school bureaucrats who desperately want to avoid admitting how terrible things have become under their administration. Tell the truth. Accentuate the negative. Maybe some parents will then pull their children out of the system.

Sixth, do whatever you can to get the schools to submit to lots of standardized tests—the more, the better. You need statistical proof of the decline of your local schools, and there is probably lots of decline! If the results show that your schools are falling below the national average, focus all the public attention you can on the collapsing quality of education in your local schools. Keep reminding parents how bad things are becoming. Maybe they will pull their children out of the system.

Seventh, try to get the votes on the board for a total financial audit. If there was an audit recently, then insist on another one by an outside firm. This costs money, but in institutions that cost as much as schools do, the auditors need auditors. It will paralyze the bureaucrats with fear, especially if they are crooked.

The school bureaucrats will hate you. The sports fanatics will hate you. So what? Your job is not to get them to like you. Your job is to represent the interests of the students and the taxpayers. You can do both by cutting costs, tightening up on school procedures, and giving raises only to high-merit (B and A "average") teachers.

Who are these teachers? Find out.

Grading the Teachers

Try to get the board to impose a merit pay system on teachers. This will throw panic into the hearts of third-rate teachers. Maybe they will quit.

Who knows how well a given teacher teaches? The honor roll (B's or better) students know. The elite scholarship society (A- or better) knows even better. Maybe you can get the board to allow these top students to rate teachers on a form provided by the board. If necessary, get the recently graduated seniors to fill in the forms. Have them rate each teacher on an A through F basis on (1) lectures, (2) ability to answer questions, (3) fairness in grading, (4) the preparation of the student for his college board exams. Have the students attach a photocopy of their SAT or ACT scores on the sheet, but not their names.

This system works for high school graduates. What about grade school teachers and junior high teachers? Just go to the record books. The computer can do it, or be programmed to do it. See the grade point averages of those students at the next level up. Check out the grades of the first-year junior high students to see how well the elementary school teachers are doing. Check out the grades of first-year high school students to see how the junior high school teachers are doing.

If some teachers consistently produce above-average or below-average students, take appropriate action.

When these teachers are ready for raises, start using student ratings to evaluate who deserves a raise and who should be encouraged to seek employment elsewhere.

Anyone who says that students are not competent to rate teachers has forgotten how well he knew when he was a senior. By having the students include a photocopy of their board scores (without names), you can find out if the poorer prepared students rate poor teachers well and hard teachers poorly. But I can pretty well assure you that most students going to college will agree on which teachers did *their* homework.

I know of a person who is presently developing the appropriate computer program to rate teachers. Contact him at

Grading Teachers
P.O. Box 8204
Ft. Worth, TX 76124

You will then push the board to make these "report cards" available to students, parents, and the press. If the schools were truly free market institutions, parents would be given the right to select the teacher of their children. They would have to pay extra to get popular, competent teachers. This would be a true merit pay system. This is one reason why universities pay high salaries to famous scholars; these scholars attract high quality students to the campus. The reason why high schools and elementary schools do not imitate colleges, or profit-seeking businesses, is that parents officially have no choice in selecting teachers, and teachers are not paid in terms of parental choices. In short, *there is no accountability.*

Teachers will oppose such a system. They will say, "You're making this a popularity contest among students. It will cause grade inflation." But for the last generation, we have had greater grade inflation than ever before. This has led to lawsuits against school districts by outraged parents of functionally illiterate students.

What Christians on the school board should do is to call for accountability in order to head off these lawsuits. How? By getting rid of the incompetents before they ruin more students and hand out more B's and A's to these ruined students.

The public school bureaucrats do not want accountability. These schools were invented in order to create a legalized monopoly that would not permit economic accountability. That is what state-run monopolies are all about. Any attempt to impose a system of merit pay, especially pay based on the evaluation of teacher competence by students, and most especially pay based on the published results of student evaluations, will create a revolt among the teachers. It will lead to a confrontation with the teacher union. Here is how to win such a confrontation.

Gaining the Cooperation of the Teachers Union

Teachers unions talk "professionalism" and "high quality education," but they will invariably fight any school board that attempts to impose merit pay standards, especially merit based on the opinion of those who are the 12-year victims, the graduates. They will try to create havoc for the board that actively pursues merit pay for good teachers.

Here is a sure-fire way to create havoc right back. You are going to do what school boards never, ever have the guts to do. You are going to find out the *true market value of the teachers.* Place an inexpensive advertisement in the college newspaper of the largest college or university in your state. If necessary, you pay for it personally. The ad should say:

Wanted: School Teachers
Starting Salary: $12,000 a year
Your Unified School District
P.O. Box [the School Board's]

If you can get the board to go along, be open about the district that is making the offer. If you can't, then have a friend in another school district nearby rent a post office box. Don't mention any district in your ad. Instead, use his post office box number. What you are after initially is a stack of inquiries.

Maybe $12,000 is too high a salary level. Maybe it is too low. You can gain access to district records and check out what the average teacher's salary is locally. Make sure that the salary you advertise is at least ten percent under the *lowest* salary that the district is paying to *new* teachers at the appropriate grade level.

You will get a stack of inquiries. The more you advertise, the more you will receive. Then send out applications. You will get back a pile of them. These completed application forms are the key to your strategy.

Remember, these applicants are young. They probably have no families or small ones. They are earning practically nothing. Dad is about to cut off their education money. Maybe they owe money on a school loan. They need a job. They are mobile. They will work for far lower wages than your local, mortgage-burdened teachers are presently working for. They will probably work far harder for several years than the district's cynical, battle-weary veteran teachers are willing to work. Test the market. Then prove your point.

Here is your point: local teachers are *way* overpaid. Prove it. Take in this stack of completed job applications—the higher the stack, the better—the next time the district's teachers ask the board for a pay raise, or threaten a strike if the district imposes teacher rating by students.

"Folks," you will say, "we have applicants here for your jobs. There are five [ten, twenty, whatever] applicants for every job in the district. These are all qualified teachers. They are all willing to work for at least 10 percent under the lowest-paid teacher presently on the payroll. We suggest that you avoid making unreasonable demands."

You will shock them into paralysis. No school board ever does this to the local teacher union, but it is the obvious response. The board is just doing what any house buyer or car buyer does. It does a bit of comparative shopping before it signs a contract.

If the teachers continue to squawk, don't rehire the untenured ones. Hire replacements from the list of applicants. This will send a terrifying message to tenured teachers, and it will get off on the right foot with the newly hired ones. They will know just why they got their jobs. Next year, everyone will get the message. They will know that the board means business.

What about the tenured ones? Legally, they cannot be fired. But they can be subtly pressured to quit. Check the existing contracts. There are always loopholes. Do some of them teach summer school? Are these summer teaching jobs guaranteed in the existing contracts? If not, don't hire them next summer; use untenured teachers to teach summer school. After all, they are paid far less during the year; they need the extra money. "All those in favor of squeezing these bright, young teachers, please stand up!" These untenured teachers will not be in a position next year to make unreasonable demands.

Your goal is legally to pressure the tenured, higher-paid, C-rated (or below) faculty members into other lines of work, or into other school districts. Make them do every crummy job that the contracts allow the board to get away with. If they teach seniors, shift them to teaching freshmen. If they teach honor students, assign them to teach remedials (commonly referred to by teachers as "the droolers.") Make it clear to them that they will never teach another B or A student, and that they will never again get a raise. Never say so publicly. Never say so in a letter. Just hold firm to the program. The program is (1) larger classes, (2) lower budgets, (3) untenured teachers, (4) merit pay.

Remember, the nation is in an educational crisis. We are a "Nation at Risk" according to the President's Commission. We hear it all the time, mostly in propaganda hand-outs by teacher unions seeking more money and smaller classrooms. "Something needs to be done!" we are told. So *do* something. "Everyone must make sacrifices!" Especially tenured teachers who are not rated A or B by graduates.

The more untenured, lower-paid, recently hired teachers are employed in your schools, the lower their wages need to be. The board can then just "hold the line on wages," year after year, resisting all wage increases, and allow inflation to cut salaries.

Then wait for students to tell you who is good.

If the union ever goes on strike, issue a press release. Call a press conference. Take your stack of applications to the local television station. Inform the media that local teachers are simply being unreasonable in their wage demands. "The taxpayers of this city deserve a break!" They do, too.

Who knows, maybe the strikers will shut down the whole public school system. Maybe they will tie up the district in court. If so, you have done your work well.

Our ultimate, long-term goal is simple: *"Shut it down!"* Legally, of course. Get the bureaucrats to fire the first shot.

By the way, you can use this same strategy against any bureaucrat. If you want to underbid them, just advertise job openings in professional newspapers or journals that circulate in places like New York City, Detroit, or Chicago. Don't advertise a salary. Most people live in areas that have a lower cost of living than these places, or at least a better environment. When you get inquiries, send out an application blank with a copy of the real estate section of the local classified ads of the newspaper. Also send out a Chamber of Commerce flyer on recreation facilities in the area. You will get plenty of applications from discouraged inner-city vice principals and principals. You might even get a school superintendent or two.

They will work cheaper.

Time-Wasting Reform Efforts

We possess severely limited resources. We cannot fight every possible battle, let alone win all of them. We dare not act as though we can win them. We must therefore learn to pick and choose our battles. I would strongly recommend not picking the following ones.

Prayer in State Schools (but not Colleges)

Forget about this project. It is totally inappropriate, except as a hook to get Christians involved in a dead-end political project. Except as a way to teach Christians that the schools are today totally in control by the enemy, it is a waste of time. Also, there is almost no active, sacrificial political support for such a project.

I agree entirely with J. Gresham Machen [GRESSum MAY-chin], the leader of the Bible-believing Christians against the modernists from 1923 until his death on New Year's Day in 1937. He spoke to Christian teachers in 1933. He warned them against Bible reading in the public schools. He also warned against public prayer.

> For my part, I have no hesitation in saying that I am strongly opposed to it. I think I am just about as opposed to the reading of the Bible in state-controlled schools as any atheist could be. . . . [T]he Bible still may be so read as to obscure and even contradict its true message. When, for example, the great and glorious promises of the Bible to the redeemed children of God are read as though they belonged of right to man as man, have we not an attack upon the very heart and core of the Bible's teaching? What could be more terrible, for example, from the Christian point of view, than the reading of the Lord's Prayer to non-Christian children, as though they could use it without becoming Christians, as though persons who have never been purchased by the blood of Christ could possibly say to God, "Our Father, which art in Heaven"? The truth is that a garbled Bible may be a falsified Bible; and when any hope is held out to lost humanity from the so-called ethical portions of the Bible apart from its great redemptive core, then the Bible is represented as saying the direct opposite of what it really says.[1]

------

1. Reprinted in *The Journal of Christian Reconstruction*, V (Summer, 1978), p. 185ff.

Creationism in State Schools (but not Colleges)

The other will-o-the-wisp these days is getting six-day creationism taught in the science classes. What a preposterous goal! What a dream that absorbs our money and time! The humanists will never allow it. They run the schools, and they will never allow it. Equal time for creationism is against their religion. Canadian Professor Michael Ruse has spoken for all evolutionists, and they control the curriculum in state school biology courses:

> I believe Creationism is wrong: totally, utterly, and absolutely wrong. I would go further. There are degrees of being wrong. The Creationists are at the bottom of the scale. They pull every trick in the book to justify their position. Indeed, at times, they verge right over into the downright dishonest. Scientific Creationism is not just wrong: it is ludicrously implausible. It is a grotesque parody of human thought, and a downright misuse of human intelligence. In short, to the Believer, it is an insult to God.[2]

> Under no circumstances would I let Creationist ideas into [tax-financed school] biology classes, or anywhere else where they might be taken by students as possible frameworks of belief. I would not give Creationism equal time. I would not give it any time.[3]

The courts constantly uphold their monopoly over curriculum. When we have enough political clout to restructure the courts, we will also have enough clout to abolish tax-supported education.

We are wasting our time on such suicidal school reform projects. Better to put our efforts into building Christian schools and electing school boards that will steadily reduce the money going to public education.

Summary

There must be no compromise with the public schools by

---

2. Michael Ruse, *Darwinism Defended: A Guide to the Evolution Controversies* (Reading, Massachusetts: Addison-Wesley, 1982), p. 303.

3. *Ibid.*, p. 321.

Christian parents. They must not send their children to such schools. The first step is to pull your children out of the public schools. All reform programs begin here.

Next, we need to cut off the funding for public schools, election by election. Fight all increases in property taxes. Vote no on every school bond issue. Organize others to do the same.

Next, do whatever possible to reduce political pressure against private education. Fight every zoning commission decision against Christian schools. Fight every decision of state or local school authorities to register, test, or in any other way infringe on the authority of parents or private schools.

Run for the school board. Impose a program of cutting expenses. Impose a program of full accountability of school officials and teachers to the public. Get a merit pay system running. Get a program of teacher evaluation by students. Represent taxpayers and students. Nobody else does.

RECOMMENDED READING LIST

There are many places to get help in educating your children. If you are teaching your children at home, I recommend you contact Christian Liberty Academy Satellite Schools (CLASS), 502 West Euclid Avenue, Arlington Heights, Illinois 60004. Their phone number is 312-259-8736. They have a home school program enrolling thousands of children. Those teaching in the home will find Samuel L. Blumenfeld's book, *How to Tutor*, useful. It can be purchased from Mott Media, P.O. Box 236, Milford, Michigan 48042.

Parents teaching in the home will find any of the books listed below helpful. They can be purchased from Fairfax Christian Bookstore, P.O. Box 6941, Tyler, Texas 75711. Their phone number is 214-581-0677 or 214-561-7944. Request a catalog. Many other fine books and materials are available through them.

Books and Materials

The Messianic Character of American Education, by Dr. Rousas J. Rushdoony, traces educational philosophy from Horace Mann down to the present. Rushdoony shows how humanist educators look upon the public schools as the new messiah, designed to save mankind from all its ills. Rushdoony is an important writer and thinker who has authored over 30 books. This book is widely used in conservative Christian colleges.

Child Abuse in the Classroom, edited by Phyllis Schlafly, consists of excerpts from the testimony of parents and students before the United States Department of Education in connection with the protection of pupil rights. If you want to read some firsthand testimony of what is going on in the government schools, this book is for you. Don't read it before going to bed. Read it just before going to your next PTA meeting if your kids are still in the government schools.

An Acorn in My Hand, by Ethel Bouldin, is especially recommended for teachers and parents who teach at home. It is great for phonics and beginning reading. It is so popular that it has gone through several printings in the past few years.

The Philosophy of the Christian Curriculum, by Dr. Rousas J. Rushdoony, delves into a Biblical approach to teaching in various subject areas.

Parents' Rights, is by John W. Whitehead, a constitutional lawyer who is involved with protecting the rights of parents to educate their children.

I highly recommend the books of Gary North, Ph.D. Dr. North is a brilliant and lucid writer. He is the outstanding scholar and writer in the world in the area of Biblical economics. North is also very practical. His newsletter, *Remnant Review*, is helpful to those who want to improve their incomes as well as to understand issues of the day. Write to P.O. Box 8204, Ft. Worth, Texas 76112 for further information.

Starting a School

I wrote a comprehensive manual, *How to Establish and Operate a Successful Christian School*, in 1975. I spent over five years on the book while operating a Christian School. It has chapters dealing with organization, financing, government regulations, facilities, curriculum, faculty, transportation, advertising, admissions, administration, class scheduling, discipline, report cards, etc. The book is very detailed. There are 40 pages on curriculum alone, with information on what books to use and where to get them.

I have been told that the chapter on finances alone is worth the price of the book. This manual is recommended for those who are serious about starting a Christian school. The book is available from Fairfax Christian Bookstore, P.O. Box 6941, Tyler, Texas 75711. The Fairfax Christian Bookstore features a Starter Kit for Christian Schools which includes the manual above. Write to them for further details.

SCRIPTURE INDEX

SUBJECT INDEX

Abel, 42
abolish the public schools, 76, 152, 159, 171
abortion, xii, 11-12, 15, 30, 87
abortion mentality, 36
Abraham, 13, 51
academic crisis, 4
academic results, poor, 57
accreditation, 96-97
  American Bar Association, 100-1
  curriculum, 99
  danger in, 99
  educational philosophy, 99
  hardships of, 100
  law schools and, 100
  Michigan, Holland, 100
  Oral Roberts University, 101
  private agency of, 99
  religious act of, 97
  requirements for, 100
Acropolis, 68
ACT, 165
Adam, 31, 36, 51, 76, 84, 88, 133
Adam, sin of, 31
AIDS, xvii
American fundamentalism, 157
American Bar Association, 100-1
American Revolution, 75
anti-family policies, 54
Apostles' Creed, 96
atheists, radical, xi, 86
Athens, ancient, 68, 81

Babylon, ancient, 48
baptism, 13

Barzun, Jacques, 5
basic institutions: family, church, state, 96
Bastiat, 37
battle zone, 34
Berean Christians, 25
Bergman, Ingmar, 16
Bible, xi, xiii, xiv, 83-84, 153
Bible as literature, 83
Bible reading in public schools, 170
Bible, the textbook of Christian schools, 18
Biblical authority, 55
Biblical case against public schools, 122
Biblical law, 95
Biblical morality, 83
Biblical solutions, ix
Biblical view of education, xv
The Big Lie, 28, 29, 34
birth control devices, 87
blood of Christ, 32
Bob Jones University, 110
bond elections, defeat of, 158-59
bonds, 113
bonds, tax-exempt, 114
busing, forced, xvii, 65
"By what standard?", 88

Caesar, 12
Caesar, stop tithing our children to, 154
Cain, 42
Caleb, 91

177

WHAT ARE BIBLICAL BLUEPRINTS?
by Gary North

How many times have you heard this one?

"The Bible isn't a textbook of . . ."

You've heard it about as many times as you've heard this one:

"The Bible doesn't provide blueprints for . . ."

The odd fact is that some of the people who assure you of this are Christians. Nevertheless, if you ask them, "Does the Bible have answers for the problems of life?" you'll get an unqualified "yes" for an answer.

Question: If the Bible isn't a textbook, and if it doesn't provide blueprints, then just how, specifically and concretely, does it provide answers for life's problems? Either it answers real-life problems, or it doesn't.

In short: *Does the Bible make a difference?*

Let's put it another way. If a mass revival at last hits this nation, and if millions of people are regenerated by God's grace through faith in the saving work of Jesus Christ at Calvary, will this change be visible in the way the new converts run their lives? Will their politics change, their business dealings change, their families change, their family budgets change, and their church membership change?

In short: Will conversion make a visible difference in our personal lives? If not, why not?

Second, two or three years later, will Congress be voting for a different kind of defense policy, foreign relations policy, environmental policy, immigration policy, monetary policy, and so forth?

Will the Federal budget change? If not, why not?

In short: Will conversion to Christ make a visible difference in our civilization? If not, why not?

The Great Commission

What the Biblical Blueprints Series is attempting to do is to outline what some of that visible difference in our culture ought to be. The authors are attempting to set forth, in clear language, *fundamental Biblical principles* in numerous specific areas of life. The authors are not content to speak in vague generalities. These books not only set forth explicit principles that are found in the Bible and derived from the Bible, they also offer specific practical suggestions about what things need to be changed, and how Christians can begin programs that will produce these many changes.

The authors see the task of American Christians just as the Puritans who came to North America in the 1630's saw their task: *to establish a city on a hill* (Matthew 5:14). The authors want to see a Biblical reconstruction of the United States, so that it can serve as an example to be followed all over the world. They believe that God's principles are tools of evangelism, to bring the nations to Christ. The Bible promises us that these principles will produce such good fruit that the whole world will marvel (Deuteronomy 4:5-8). When nations begin to marvel, they will begin to soften to the message of the gospel. What the authors are calling for is *comprehensive revival*—a revival that will transform everything on earth.

In other words, the authors are calling Christians to obey God and take up the Great Commission: to *disciple* (discipline) all the nations of the earth (Matthew 28:19).

What each author argues is that there are God-required principles of thought and practice in areas that some people today believe to be outside the area of "religion." What Christians should know by now is that *nothing* lies outside religion. God is judging all of our thoughts and acts, judging our institutions, and working through human history to bring this world to a final judgment.

We present the case that God offers *comprehensive salvation* — regeneration, healing, restoration, and the obligation of total social reconstruction — because the world is in *comprehensive sin.*

To judge the world it is obvious that God has to have standards. If there were no absolute standards, there could be no earthly judgment, and no final judgment because men could not be held accountable.

(Warning: these next few paragraphs are very important. They are the base of the entire Blueprints series. It is important that you understand my reasoning. I really believe that if you understand it, you will agree with it.)

To argue that God's standards don't apply to everything is to argue that sin hasn't affected and infected everything. To argue that God's Word doesn't give us a revelation of God's requirements for us is to argue that we are flying blind as Christians. It is to argue that there are *zones of moral neutrality* that God will not judge, either today or at the day of judgment, because these zones somehow are *outside His jurisdiction.* In short, "no law-no jurisdiction."

But if God *does* have jurisdiction over the whole universe, which is what every Christian believes, then there must be universal standards by which God executes judgment. The authors of this series argue for God's *comprehensive judgment,* and we declare His *comprehensive salvation.* We therefore are presenting a few of His *comprehensive blueprints.*

The Concept of Blueprints

An architectural blueprint gives us the structural requirements of a building. A blueprint isn't intended to tell the owner where to put the furniture or what color to paint the rooms. A blueprint does place limits on where the furniture and appliances should be put — laundry here, kitchen there, etc. — but it doesn't take away our personal options based on personal taste. A blueprint just specifies what must be done during construction for the building to do its job and to survive the test of time. It gives direction to the contractor. Nobody wants to be on the twelfth floor of a building that collapses.

Today, we are unquestionably on the twelfth floor, and maybe even the fiftieth. Most of today's "buildings" (institutions) were designed by humanists, for use by humanists, but paid for mostly by Christians (investments, donations, and taxes). These "buildings" aren't safe. Christians (and a lot of non-Christians) now are hearing the creaking and groaning of these tottering buildings. Millions of people have now concluded that it's time to: (1) call in a totally new team of foundation and structural specialists to begin a complete renovation, or (2) hire the original contractors to make at least temporary structural modifications until we can all move to safer quarters, or (3) call for an emergency helicopter team because time has just about run out, and the elevators aren't safe either.

The writers of this series believe that the first option is the wise one: Christians need to rebuild the foundations, using the Bible as their guide. This view is ignored by those who still hope and pray for the third approach: God's helicopter escape. Finally, those who have faith in minor structural repairs don't tell us what or where these hoped-for safe quarters are, or how humanist contractors are going to build them any safer next time.

Why is it that some Christians say that God hasn't drawn up any blueprints? If God doesn't give us blueprints, then who does? If God doesn't set the permanent standards, then who does? If God hasn't any standards to judge men by, then who judges man?

The humanists' answer is inescapable: *man* does—autonomous, design-it-yourself, do-it-yourself man. Christians call this man-glorifying religion the religion of humanism. It is amazing how many Christians until quite recently have believed humanism's first doctrinal point, namely, that God has not established permanent blueprints for man and man's institutions. Christians who hold such a view of God's law serve as *humanism's chaplains*.

Men are God's appointed "contractors." We were never supposed to draw up the blueprints, but we *are* supposed to execute them, in history and then after the resurrection. Men have been given dominion on the earth to subdue it for God's glory. "So God created man in His own image; in the image of God He created him; male and female He created them. Then God blessed them, and God said to them, 'Be fruitful and multiply; fill the earth and subdue it; have dominion over the fish of the sea, over the birds of the air, and over every living thing that moves on the earth'" (Genesis 1:27-28).

Christians about a century ago decided that God never gave them the responsibility to do any building (except for churches). That was just what the humanists had been waiting for. They immediately stepped in, took over the job of contractor ("Someone has to do it!"), and then announced that they would also be in charge of drawing up the blueprints. We can see the results of a similar assertion in Genesis, chapter 11: the tower of Babel. Do you remember God's response to that particular humanistic public works project?

Never Be Embarrassed By the Bible

This sounds simple enough. Why should Christians be embarrassed by the Bible? But they *are* embarrassed . . . millions of them. The humanists have probably done more to slow down the spread of the gospel by convincing Christians to be embarrassed by the Bible than by any other strategy they have adopted.

Test your own thinking. Answer this question: "Is God mostly a God of love or mostly a God of wrath?" Think about it before you answer.

It's a trick question. The Biblical answer is: "God is equally a God of love and a God of wrath." But Christians these days will generally answer almost automatically, "God is mostly a God of love, not wrath."

Now in their hearts, they know this answer can't be true. God sent His Son to the cross to die. His own Son! That's how much God hates sin. That's wrath with a capital "W."

But why did He do it? Because He loves His Son, and those who follow His Son. So, you just can't talk about the wrath of God without talking about the love of God, and vice versa. The cross is the best proof we have: God is both wrathful and loving. Without the fires of hell as the reason for the cross, the agony of Jesus Christ on the cross was a mistake, a case of drastic overkill.

What about heaven and hell? We know from John's vision of the day of judgment, "Death and Hades [hell] were cast into the lake of fire. This is the second death. And anyone not found written in the Book of Life was cast into the lake of fire" (Revelation 20:14-15).

Those whose names are in the Book of Life spend eternity with God in their perfect, sin-free, resurrected bodies. The Bible calls this the New Heaven and the New Earth.

Now, which is more eternal, the lake of fire, or the New Heaven and the New Earth? Obviously, they are both eternal. So, God's wrath is equally ultimate with His love throughout eternity. *Christians all admit this*, but sometimes only under extreme pressure. And that is precisely the problem.

For over a hundred years, theological liberals have blathered on and on about the love of God. But when you ask them, "What about hell?" they start dancing verbally. If you press them, they eventually deny the existence of eternal judgment. We *must* understand: they have no doctrine of the total love of God because they have no doctrine of the total wrath of God. They can't really understand what it is that God in His grace offers us in Christ because they refuse to admit what eternal judgment tells us about the character of God.

The doctrine of eternal fiery judgment is by far the most unacceptable doctrine in the Bible, as far as hell-bound humanists are concerned. They can't believe that Christians can believe in such a horror. But we do. We must. This belief is the foundation of Christian evangelism. It is the motivation for Christian foreign missions. We shouldn't be surprised that the God-haters would like us to drop this doctrine. When Christians believe it, they make too much trouble for God's enemies.

So if we believe in this doctrine, the doctrine above all others that ought to embarrass us before humanists, then why do we start to squirm when God-hating people ask us: "Well, what kind of God would require the death penalty? What kind of God would send a plague (or other physical judgment) on people, the way He sent one on the Israelites, killing 70,000 of them, even though they had done nothing wrong, just because David had conducted a military census in peacetime (2 Samuel 24:10-16)? What kind of God sends AIDS?" The proper answer: "The God of the Bible, *my* God."

Compared to the doctrine of eternal punishment, what is some two-bit judgment like a plague? Compared to eternal screaming agony in the lake of fire, without hope of escape, what is the death penalty? The liberals try to embarrass us about these earthly "down payments" on God's final judgment because they want to rid the world of the idea of final judgment. So they insult the character of God, and also the character of Christians, by sneering at the Bible's account of who God is, what He has done in history, and what He requires from men.

Are you tired of their sneering? I know I am.

Nothing in the Bible should be an embarrassment to any Christian. We may not know for certain precisely how some Biblical truth or historic event should be properly applied in our day, but every historic record, law, announcement, prophecy, judgment, and warning in the Bible is the very Word of God, and is not to be flinched at by anyone who calls himself by Christ's name.

We must never doubt that whatever God did in the Old Testament era, the Second Person of the Trinity also did. God's counsel and judgments are not divided. We must be careful not to regard Jesus Christ as a sort of "unindicted co-conspirator" when we read the Old Testament. "For whoever is ashamed of Me and My words in this adulterous and sinful generation, of him the Son of Man also will be ashamed when He comes in the glory of His Father with the holy angels" (Mark 8:38).

My point here is simple. If we as Christians can accept what is a very hard principle of the Bible, that Christ was a blood sacrifice for our individual sins, then we shouldn't flinch at accepting any of the rest of God's principles. As we joyfully accepted His salvation, so we must joyfully embrace all of His principles that affect any and every area of our lives.

The Whole Bible

When, in a court of law, the witness puts his hand on the Bible and swears to tell the truth, the whole truth, and nothing but the truth, so help him God, he thereby swears on the Word of God—the *whole* Word of God, and *nothing but* the Word of God. The Bible is a unit. It's a "package deal." The New Testament doesn't overturn the Old Testament; it's a *commentary* on the Old Testament. It tells us how to use the Old Testament properly in the period after the death and resurrection of Israel's messiah, God's Son.

Jesus said: "Do not think that I came to destroy the Law or the Prophets. I did not come to destroy but to fulfill. For assuredly, I say to you, till heaven and earth pass away, one jot or one tittle will by no means pass from the law till all is fulfilled. Whoever therefore breaks one of the least of these commandments, and teaches men to do so, shall be called least in the kingdom of heaven; but whoever does and teaches them, he shall be called great in the kingdom of heaven" (Matthew 5:17-19). The Old Testament isn't a discarded first draft of God's Word. It isn't "God's Word emeritus."

Dominion Christianity teaches that there are four covenants under God, meaning four kinds of *vows* under God: personal (individual), and the three institutional covenants: ecclesiastical (the church), civil (governments), and family. All other human institutions (business, educational, charitable, etc.) are to one degree or other under the jurisdiction of these four covenants. No single covenant is absolute; therefore, no single institution is all-powerful. Thus, Christian liberty is *liberty under God and God's law.*

Christianity therefore teaches pluralism, but a very special kind of pluralism: plural institutions under God's comprehensive law. It does not teach a pluralism of law structures, or a pluralism of moralities, for as we will see shortly, this sort of ultimate pluralism (as distinguished from *institutional* pluralism) is always either polytheistic or humanistic. Christian people are required to take dominion over the earth by means of all these God-ordained institutions, not just the church, or just the state, or just the family.

The kingdom of God includes every human institution, and every aspect of life, for all of life is under God and is governed by His unchanging principles. All of life is under God and God's principles because God intends to *judge* all of life *in terms of* His principles.

In this structure of *plural governments*, the institutional churches serve as *advisors* to the other institutions (the Levitical function), but the churches can only pressure individual leaders through the threat of excommunication. As a restraining factor on unwarranted church authority, an unlawful excommunication by one local church or denomination is always subject to review by the others if and when the excommunicated person seeks membership elsewhere. Thus, each of the three covenantal institutions is to be run under God, as interpreted by its lawfully elected or ordained leaders, with the advice of the churches, not the compulsion.

Majority Rule

Just for the record, the authors aren't in favor of imposing some sort of top-down bureaucratic tyranny in the name of Christ. The kingdom of God requires a bottom-up society. The bottom-up Christian society rests ultimately on the doctrine of *self*-government under God. It's the humanist view of society that promotes top-down bureaucratic power.

The authors are in favor of evangelism and missions leading to a widespread Christian revival, so that the great mass of earth's inhabitants will place themselves under Christ's protection, and voluntarily use His covenantal principles for self-government. Christian reconstruction begins with personal conversion to Christ and self-government under God's principles, then spreads to others through revival, and only later brings comprehensive changes in civil law, when the vast majority of voters voluntarily agree to live under Biblical blueprints.

Let's get this straight: Christian reconstruction depends on majority rule. Of course, the leaders of the Christian reconstructionist movement expect a majority eventually to accept Christ as savior. If this doesn't happen, then Christians must be content with only partial reconstruction, and only partial blessings from

God. It isn't possible to ramrod God's blessings from the top down, unless you're God. Only humanists think that man is God. All we're trying to do is get the ramrod away from them, and melt it down. The melted ramrod could then be used to make a great grave marker for humanism: "The God That Failed."

The Continuing Heresy of Dualism

Many (of course, not all!) of the objections to the material in this book series will come from people who have a worldview that is very close to an ancient church problem: dualism. A lot of well-meaning Christian people are dualists, although they don't even know what it is.

Dualism teaches that the world is inherently divided: spirit vs. matter, or law vs. mercy, or mind vs. matter, or nature vs. grace. What the Bible teaches is that this world is divided *ethically* and *personally*: Satan vs. God, right vs. wrong. The conflict between God and Satan will end at the final judgment. Whenever Christians substitute some other form of dualism for ethical dualism, they fall into heresy and suffer the consequences. That's what has happened today. We are suffering from revived versions of ancient heresies.

Marcion's Dualism

The Old Testament was written by the same God who wrote the New Testament. There were not two Gods in history, meaning there was no dualism or radical split between the two testamental periods. There is only one God, in time and eternity.

This idea has had opposition throughout church history. An ancient two-Gods heresy was first promoted in the church about a century after Christ's crucifixion, and the church has always regarded it as just that, a heresy. It was proposed by a man named Marcion. Basically, this heresy teaches that there are two completely different law systems in the Bible: Old Testament law and New Testament law (or non-law). But Marcion took the logic of his position all the way. He argued that two law systems means two Gods. The God of wrath wrote the Old Testament, and the God of mercy wrote the New Testament. In short: "two laws-two Gods."

Many Christians still believe something dangerously close to Marcionism: not a two-Gods view, exactly, but a God-who-changed-all-His-rules sort of view. They begin with the accurate teaching that the ceremonial laws of the Old Testament were fulfilled by Christ, and therefore that the *unchanging principles* of Biblical worship are *applied differently* in the New Testament. But then they erroneously conclude that the whole Old Testament system of civil law was dropped by God, and *nothing Biblical was put in its place*. In other words, God created a sort of vacuum for state law.

This idea turns civil law-making over to Satan. In our day, this means that civil law-making is turned over to humanists. *Christians have unwittingly become the philosophical allies of the humanists with respect to civil law.* With respect to their doctrine of the state, therefore, most Christians hold what is in effect a two-Gods view of the Bible.

Gnosticism's Dualism

Another ancient heresy that is still with us is gnosticism. It became a major threat to the early church almost from the beginning. It was also a form of dualism, a theory of a radical split. The gnostics taught that the split is between evil matter and good spirit. Thus, their goal was to escape this material world through other-worldly exercises that punish the body. They believed in *retreat from the world of human conflicts and responsibility.* Some of these ideas got into the church, and people started doing ridiculous things. One "saint" sat on a platform on top of a pole for several decades. This was considered very spiritual. (Who fed him? Who cleaned up after him?)

Thus, many Christians came to view "the world" as something permanently outside the kingdom of God. They believed that this hostile, forever-evil world cannot be redeemed, reformed, and reconstructed. Jesus didn't really die for it, and it can't be healed. At best, it can be subdued by power (maybe). This dualistic view of the world vs. God's kingdom narrowly restricted any earthly manifestation of God's kingdom. Christians who were influenced by gnosticism concluded that God's kingdom refers only to the institutional church. They argued that the institutional church is the *only* manifestation of God's kingdom.

This led to two opposite and equally evil conclusions. *First*, power religionists ("salvation through political power") who accepted this definition of God's kingdom tried to put the institutional church in charge of everything, since it is supposedly "the only manifestation of God's kingdom on earth." To subdue the supposedly unredeemable world, which is forever outside the kingdom, the institutional church has to rule with the sword. A single, monolithic institutional church then gives orders to the state, and the state must without question enforce these orders with the sword. The hierarchy of the institutional church concentrates political and economic power. *What then becomes of liberty?*

Second, escape religionists ("salvation is exclusively internal") who also accepted this narrow definition of the kingdom sought refuge from the evil world of matter and politics by fleeing to hide inside the institutional church, an exclusively "spiritual kingdom," now narrowly defined. They abandoned the world to evil tyrants. *What then becomes of liberty?* What becomes of the idea of God's progressive restoration of all things under Jesus Christ? What, finally, becomes of the idea of Biblical dominion?

When Christians improperly narrow their definition of the kingdom of God, the visible influence of this comprehensive kingdom (both spiritual and institutional at the same time) begins to shrivel up. The first heresy leads to tyranny *by* the church, and the second heresy leads to tyranny *over* the church. Both of these narrow definitions of God's kingdom destroy the liberty of the responsible Christian man, self-governed under God and God's law.

Zoroaster's Dualism

The last ancient pagan idea that still lives on is also a variant of dualism: matter vs. spirit. It teaches that God and Satan, good and evil, are forever locked in combat, and that good never triumphs over evil. The Persian religion of Zoroastrianism has held such a view for over 2,500 years. The incredibly popular "Star Wars" movies were based on this view of the world: the "dark" side of "the force" against its "light" side. In modern versions of this ancient dualism, the "force" is usually seen as itself impersonal: individuals personalize either the dark side or the light side by "plugging into" its power.

There are millions of Christians who have adopted a very pessimistic version of this dualism, though not in an impersonal form. God's kingdom is battling Satan's, and God's is losing. History isn't going to get better. In fact, things are going to get a lot worse externally. Evil will visibly push good into the shadows. The church is like a band of soldiers who are surrounded by a huge army of Indians. "We can't win boys, so hold the fort until Jesus comes to rescue us!"

That doesn't sound like Abraham, Moses, Joshua, Gideon, and David, does it? Christians read to their children one of the children's favorite stories, David and Goliath, yet in their own lives, millions of Christian parents really think that the Goliaths of this world are the unbeatable earthly winners. Christians haven't even picked up a stone.

Until very recently.

An Agenda for Victory

The change has come since 1980. Many Christians' thinking has shifted. Dualism, gnosticism, and "God changed His program midstream" ideas have begun to be challenged. The politicians have already begun to reckon with the consequences. Politicians are the people we pay to raise their wet index fingers in the wind to sense a shift, and they have sensed it. It scares them, too. It should.

A new vision has captured the imaginations of a growing army of registered voters. This new vision is simple: it's the old vision of Genesis 1:27-28 and Matthew 28:19-20. It's called *dominion*.

Four distinct ideas must be present in any ideology that expects to overturn the existing view of the world and the existing social order:

> A doctrine of ultimate truth (permanence)
> A doctrine of providence (confidence)
> Optimism toward the future (motivation)
> Binding comprehensive law (reconstruction)

The Marxists have had such a vision, or at least those Marxists who don't live inside the bureaucratic giants called the Soviet Union and Red China. The radical (please, not "fundamentalist") Muslims of Iran also have such a view.

Now, for the first time in over 300 years, Bible-believing Christians have rediscovered these four points in the theology of Christianity. For the first time in over 300 years, a growing number of Christians are starting to view themselves as an army on the move. This army will grow. This series is designed to help it grow. And grow tougher.

The authors of this series are determined to set the agenda in world affairs for the next few centuries. We know where the permanent answers are found: in the Bible, and *only* in the Bible. We believe that we have begun to discover at least preliminary answers to the key questions. There may be better answers, clearer answers, and more orthodox answers, but they must be found in the Bible, not at Harvard University or on the CBS Evening News.

We are self-consciously firing the opening shot. We are calling the whole Christian community to join with us in a very serious debate, just as Luther called them to debate him when he nailed the 95 theses to the church door, over four and a half centuries ago.

It is through such an exchange of ideas by those who take the Bible seriously that a nation and a civilization can be saved. There are now 5 billion people in the world. If we are to win our world (and these billions of souls) for Christ we must lift up the message of Christ by becoming the city on the hill. When the world sees the blessings by God upon a nation run by His principles, the mass conversion of whole nations to the Kingdom of our Lord will be the most incredible in of all history.

If we're correct about the God-required nature of our agenda, it will attract a dedicated following. It will produce a social transformation that could dwarf the Reformation. This time, we're not limiting our call for reformation to the institutional church.

This time, we mean business.

Fairfax Christian Bookstore
P.O. Box 6941
Tyler, TX 75711

Gentlemen:

I just finished reading Robert Thoburn's *The Children Trap*. I understand that you carry his other books, *The Christian and Politics* and *How to Establish and Operate a Successful Christian School* (a comprehensive manual). Please send me information on these, and other books that Mr. Thoburn recommends, including the famous *McGuffey Readers*.

_____
name

_____
address

_____
city, state, zip

_____
area code and phone number

☐ Please also send me information on your Starter Kit for Christian Schools, which includes Mr. Thoburn's manual.

Robert L. Thoburn
Fairfax Christian School
10521 Rosehaven Street, Suite 305
Fairfax, VA 22030

Dear Mr. Thoburn:

I just finished reading your book, *The Children Trap*. Please send me information on the services and materials which you provide for Christian education.

_____
name

_____
address

_____
city, state, zip

_____
area code and phone number

Dr. Gary North
Institute for Christian Economics
P.O. Box 8000
Tyler, TX 75711

Dear Dr. North:

I read about your organization in Robert Thoburn's book, *The Children Trap.* I understand that you publish several newsletters that are sent out for six months free of charge. I would be interested in receiving them:

☐ *Biblical Economics Today*
  Christian Reconstruction
  and Dominion Strategies

Please send any other information you have concerning your program.

_____
name

_____
address

_____
city, state, zip

_____
area code and phone number

☐ Enclosed is a tax-deductible donation to help meet expenses.

Jesus said to "Occupy till I come." But if Christians don't control the territory, they can't occupy it. They get tossed out into cultural "outer darkness," which is just exactly what the secular humanists have done to Christians in the 20th century: in education, in the arts, in entertainment, in politics, and certainly in the mainline churches and seminaries. Today, the humanists are "occupying." But they won't be for long. *Backward, Christian Soldiers?* shows you why. This is must reading for all Christians as a supplement to the *Biblical Blueprints Series*. You can obtain a copy by sending $1.00 (a $5.95 value) to:

Institute for Christian Economics
P.O. Box 8000
Tyler, TX 75703

_____

name

_____

address

_____

city, state, zip

_____   _____

area code and phone number

Dominion Press • P.O. Box 8204 • Ft. Worth, TX 76124

The *Biblical Blueprints Series* is a multi-volume book series that gives Biblical solutions for the problems facing our culture today. Each book deals with a specific topic in a simple, easy to read style such as economics, government, law, crime and punishment, welfare and poverty, taxes, money and banking, politics, the environment, retirement, and much more.

Each book can be read in one evening and will give you the basic Biblical principles on each topic. Each book concludes with three chapters on how to apply the principles in your life, the church and the nation. Every chapter is summarized so that the entire book can be absorbed in just a few minutes.

As you read these books, you will discover hundreds of new ways to serve God. Each book will show you ways that you can start to implement God's plan in your own life. As hundreds of thousands join you, and millions more begin to follow the example set, a civilization can be changed.

Why will people change their lives? Because they will see God's blessings on those who live by His Word (Deuteronomy 4:6-8).

Each title in the *Biblical Blueprints Series* is available in a deluxe paperback edition for $6.95, or a classic leatherbound edition for $14.95.

The following titles are scheduled for publication in 1986:

- Introduction to Dominion: Biblical Blueprints on Dominion
- Honest Money: Biblical Blueprints on Money and Banking
- Who Owns the Family?: Biblical Blueprints on the Family and the State
- In the Shadow of Plenty: Biblical Blueprints on Welfare and Poverty
- Liberator of the Nations: Biblical Blueprints on Political Action
- Inherit the Earth: Biblical Blueprints on Economics
- Chariots of God: Biblical Blueprints on Defense
- The Children Trap: Biblical Blueprints on Education
- Entangling Alliances: Biblical Blueprints on Foreign Policy
- Ruler of the Nations: Biblical Blueprints on Government
- Protection of the Innocent: Biblical Blueprints on Crime and Punishment

Additional Volumes of the Biblical Blueprints Series are scheduled for 1987 and 1988.

Please send more information concerning this program.

name

address

city, state, zip